CONTENTS

Principal Writers: Donald Cowey and Andrew Smith ('The Celtic View').

Career Statistics

Season	League		League Cup		Scottish Cup		Europe		Total	
	Apps	Goals	Apps	Goals	Apps	Goals	Apps	Goals	Apps	Goals
81-82	7(3)	1			2				9(3)	1
82-83	36	6	9	1	4		4		53	7
83-84	34	3	8	2	5	2	6	1	53	7
84-85	32	4	2		7	3	5	1	46	8
85-86	34	8	2	1	2		2		40	9
86-87	43	3	5	1	4		4		56	4
87-88	44	5	2		6		2		54	5
88-89	33	5	3		5		4		45	5
89-90	35	3	4	1	6	1	2		47	5
Total	298(3)	38	35	6	41	6	29	1	403(3)	51

Numbers in brackets indicate additional appearances as substitute.

The Captain Speaks...

I AM, first and foremost, a lifelong Celtic supporter. As such, I understand and share the fans' disappointment at our poor showing last season — and I assure everyone of my total commitment to turning things around and putting Celtic back in their rightful place at the forefront of Scottish and European football. It may take a little time — *but we'll get there!*

Being made Club Captain last January was a great honour, a major highlight of my career, even though it was tinged with the sadness of replacing my departed friend and team-mate, Roy Aitken. Roy was a great servant to Celtic and an immense inspiration to all around him — as was Tommy Burns, another legendary Celt who bowed out last season. Good luck to both of them!

As I look to the future in my new role, it is with enormous pride at following in the footsteps of my great-uncle, Jimmy McStay, who also captained the team in the late 1920's and early 1930's. My family is very important to me — indeed, I owe my career to the sacrifices of my parents and some of my happiest football memories are of playing in the same Celtic team as my brother Willie. Perhaps I can soon relive that experience with my younger brother Raymond, who has shown great promise in the reserves.

My first season as captain was a difficult one but that only sharpened my appetite for the challenge ahead. I am sure the added responsibility of captaincy has made me a better all-round player, despite the greater demands, both on and off the park. Hopefully, I can continue to raise my game, lead by example and let everything flow from that.

There were few highlights last season as the team suffered a crisis of confidence, which was reflected in recurring slumps at critical times. We saved our best displays for the Scottish Cup, with the fourth-round victory over Rangers and the quarter-final replay against Dunfermline Athletic, both at Celtic Park, the pick of the bunch.

So much depended on the February *Old Firm* encounter that victory was especially sweet, particularly as Celtic were given so little chance by the pundits. The gutsy performance proved that we could still play a bit and perhaps more importantly, that the traditional Celtic cup-fighting spirit was alive and well.

The Dunfermline replay was memorable for its three Celtic goals, which had been in short supply throughout the season. The entertaining, attacking football that night was gloriously topped off with a trio of goals to savour, including a fortuitous 20 yard strike from yours truly!

Sadly, a third successive Scottish Cup victory eluded us in the cruellest manner possible with that nerve-wracking *penalty shoot-out* in the final. Still, it was an exhilarating cup run which threw up the season's best moments and kept interest high right to the death.

A personal career landmark in 1990 was participating in the World Cup Finals during the summer, despite the crushing outcome and the agony of being relegated to the bench for the crucial Sweden match. The Italian setting was truly magnificent and rubbing shoulders with world-class performers such as Brazil's *Dunga*, *Alemao* and *Valdo* was an invaluable experience.

I only hope it has a long-term positive spin-off for my club form in domestic competition as I strive to lead my beloved Celtic back to the honours this great club and its marvellous support deserve.

Yes, Celtic really is *a grand old team to play for!*

Paul McStay

Great Games

CELTIC v Rangers

Scottish Cup 4th Round

IT WAS the game the cynics said would never happen . . . Celtic versus Rangers in the early rounds of the Cup! When the fourth round draw was made, the Old Firm pairing drew gasps of amazement from the assembled sponsors and SFA representatives. For it had become generally accepted that the paths of Celtic and Rangers did not cross in the early stages of the competition.

As well as creating a *final before the final* situation, the more outspoken critics had often openly suggested that there was a financial motive in keeping the two apart as long as possible. An early exit for either of the 'Big Two' would reduce future gates and devalue the rest of the competition.

However, such dubious inferences were swept aside when the draw brought Celtic and Rangers together prior to the final for the first time since 1970, with Celtic Park the venue. The shock waves reverberated round Scotland as the implications of the tie dominated the sports pages, radio and television.

Inevitable unkind inferences were made about the lack of square or heated balls in the bag resulting in such a grave error in the draw. Almost every press cartoon strip made some sarcastic reference but for Celtic this draw against their greatest rivals was no joking matter.

Rarely can such a vital contest have come at a more inopportune time for the club, with morale so desperately low. The month before the draw had seen Celtic effectively drop out of the championship race, with defeats by Dunfermline, Rangers and Dundee United, three games in which the greens failed miserably to score. Events after the cup ballot did nothing to dispel the impression of a club in the doldrums. The following Saturday brought a 1-0 home defeat by Motherwell, an abysmal performance which provoked angry crowd scenes outside the stadium. Three further draws followed in the league as Celtic searched in vain for a confidence booster before a vital match on which now rested the season's hopes of a trophy.

Meanwhile in contrast to Celtic's woes, the mood at Ibrox could hardly have been more buoyant. Sitting comfortably at the top of the league table, Rangers seemed set to grab a second title in succession. If any further pointers as to the likely outcome of the cup clash were required, Rangers had won at Celtic Park a mere six weeks previously — only their second victory at Parkhead in nine years!

The hype surrounding the immediate match build-up made it the most-talked-about Scottish Cup-tie in years. The pundits were not slow to present omens and almost to a man the press, radio and television "experts" plumped for Rangers, writing off the chances of the men from the East End of Glasgow, despite their great cup tradition.

But, as has so often been the case where Celtic are concerned, the script went out the window on the day. For Celtic, with their whole season resting on this one encounter, played like men possessed, summing up every last ounce of spirit and determination to answer their critics.

The Sunday showdown, with the whole nation watching, provided the platform the Celts required to demonstrate the form of which they were capable. That one, assured performance, lifted much of the gloom which had descended on Celtic Park.

The game was memorable mostly for the tactical midfield battle as both teams struggled for supremacy in that vital area. Celtic retained the upper hand throughout, always looking more positive and threatening in a match which presented few real chances.

The back division made a huge contribution to the stirring victory, with centre-half Paul Elliott quite outstanding. He deservedly won the Tennent's "Man-of-the-Match" award and was simply unbeatable in the air. His sterling work with fellow centre-back Derek Whyte completely snuffed out the threat of Rangers' international strike force, scarcely giving them a glimpse of goal in the entire 90 minutes.

The match was also a personal triumph for matchwinner Tommy Coyne, who scored the only goal of the game in 44 minutes. The former Dundee striker had been struggling for acceptance by the Celtic fans and had taken more than his fair share of criticism.

On the stroke of half-time, though, all was at least temporarily forgiven as Coyne earned his Celtic spurs. Winning a challenge with Rangers' John Brown, Tommy slipped a pass to fellow-striker Dariusz Dziekanowski, who switched the ball out to Joe Miller on the right. The winger steadied himself before shooting low across goal. Rangers' keeper Chris Woods could only divert the ball tantalisingly towards the onrushing Coyne, who slid in to bundle it over the line.

Thus Celtic progressed to the quarter-finals and Tommy Coyne at last earned some affection from a critical support, as the ovation which greeted his 76th minute exit clearly demonstrated.

Still blissfully unaware of the final agony to come, the fans went home ecstatic that Celtic had lived to fight another day and savouring the season's most delicious victory.

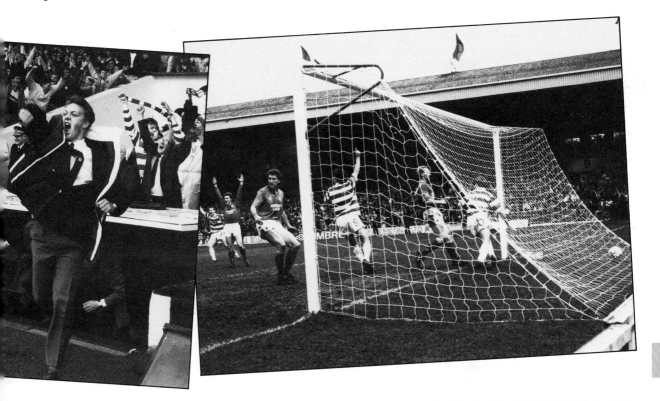

Career Statistics					
Season	League	League Cup	Scottish Cup	Europe	Total
	Appear	Appear	Appear	Appear	Appear
78-79	2				2
79-80					
80-81	36	8	5	3	52
81-82	36	6	2	2	46
82-83	36	10	4	4	54
83-84	33	11	5	6	55
84-85	34	3	6	5	48
85-86	30	3		2	35
86-87	43	5	4	4	56
87-88	32	1	5		38
88-89	26		5	2	33
89-90	36	4	6	2	48
Total	344	51	42	30	467

PAT BONNER

CELTIC supporters heading for the match last season had one steadfast source of comfort. They could rely upon goalkeeper Pat Bonner to perform heroically and regularly to make some truly remarkable saves. His consistent excellence was a source of great satisfaction for the many fans who recognised his early potential and kept faith with him through some rough times at the outset of his Celtic career.

While individual contributions are often exaggerated in overall team performance, it is fair to say that, but for Bonner, Celtic would almost certainly have been denied the Scottish Cup Final appearance which gave the supporters some lingering hope and excitement in the final weeks of the 1989/90 season. For, in the final 10 minutes of the sell-out quarter-final tie against Dunfermline Athletic at East End Park on Saturday March 17th, home striker Ross Jack connected perfectly with a close-range overhead kick. It seemed a certain winner as it flew towards the bottom right-hand corner of Bonner's goal. In a flash, though, the 'keeper pounced to make an incredible catch right on the goal-line and earn a replay at Parkhead.

A tremendous level of consistency was the main feature of his performances in a league campaign otherwise devoid of that quality.

Pat made his debut on March 17th 1979, St Patrick's Day, in a 2-1 defeat of Motherwell in the Premier Division, then lined up against the same opposition at Fir Park on April 4th, when Celtic won 4-3. Popular Englishman, Peter Latchford, reclaimed the No. 1 jersey for the remainder of that season and the whole of the subsequent one but Bonner made another appearance in Danny McGrain's testimonial match against Manchester United at Celtic Park before the start of the 1980-'81 season . . . and never looked back.

He missed only one competitive first-team game during that term and only a handful over the next six seasons. Injury saw him miss a few games in the so-successful 1987-'88 Centenary Season and still more the following one, when his absence was a significant factor in Celtic's shaky start to the campaign.

His Republic of Ireland debut came against Poland in 1981 and he earned another cap against Algeria the following year; but it was not until 1984 that he became first choice for his country.

Always a 'keeper of great shot-stopping ability, his weakness in the early days was a tendency to misjudge crosses. As time wore on his judgement became steadily sounder and he really came of age when representing his country in the 1988 European Nations' Championship finals in West Germany.

He stopped everything England could throw at him in the opening game and was very much the key to the Republic's shock 1-0 victory. The subsequent 1-1 draw with Russia meant that the Republic needed to draw their final group match with eventual winners Holland to advance to the knockout semis and final.

Once more Bonner was apparently unbeatable but just eight minutes from time, a cruel deflection presented Wim Kieft with a chance to head the winner. The scorer was in an offside position but his well-taken effort found the 'keeper stranded, dumped the Irish out of the competition and set the Dutch up for their popular success.

However, the Celtic man was considered by most observers to be the best goalkeeper in the championships and his record at international level over the past three years compares with any in the world. This fact is a source of great satisfaction for those involved with the Republic of Ireland set-up.

It also gives Celtic supporters great confidence in their final line of defence and causes them to relish the hopeful prospect of seeing Pat Bonner in goal for years to come.

Celtic v Hearts

Celtic v Rangers

JIMMY JOHNSTONE

EVERY so often, football throws up a supreme talent. Such was the talent of Jimmy Johnstone, who so captured the public imagination that even now, 15 years after he last donned the hoops, his name is still revered. To the generation privileged to watch him he was simply *'Jinky'*, a nickname which summed up a style words could not describe.

Part of his appeal lay in his appearance, which defied the popular image of a footballer. Small, frail and boyish, he sometimes seemed swamped by the jersey, as if it had been borrowed from a larger team-mate. In a game where physical power is highly-prized, Jimmy Johnstone was an unlikely hero.

He was a personality player, partly because his small stature evoked sympathy and endeared him to the fans but more importantly because of his truly magical talent on the wing. The uncanny dribbling and bewildering changes of direction could spreadeagle defences. This apparently effortless skill, while undoubtedly God-given, was the result of hours of boyhood practice. Legend has it that the young Jimmy would practise in his father's pit boots so that on match days his feet would feel light and nimble in football boots.

Jimmy made his debut in March 1963 against Kilmarnock but it was not until the arrival of Jock Stein in 1965 that the real Johnstone genius began to emerge. He established himself in season 1965-66, which brought Celtic's first championship win in 12 years. A further eight titles were to follow, in which *'Jinky'* played a major part.

He commanded a special affection from the Celtic support and such was the rapport that every fan has a favourite memory of the little redhead from Uddingston. The countless tales, some tall, some true have become part of Celtic folklore.

Memories of his playing days abound. He played only two short of 300 league matches, regularly turning in amazing performances (especially against Rangers) but he is possibly best remembered for two European triumphs.

In 1970 Celtic faced Leeds United, supposedly the best side in Europe at the time, in the European Cup. Jimmy roasted the world-rated England full-back Terry Cooper to such an extent that he was never the same player again.

A dread fear of flying spurred Johnstone to another of his greatest performances, again in the European Cup. In November 1968, Celtic met Red Star Belgrade with the first leg at home. The shrewd Jock Stein promised Jimmy that if Celtic won by four clear goals, he would not have to travel for the return leg. The match ended 5-1 with Johnstone in devastating form, beating the Yugoslavs almost singlehandedly.

If there was a flaw in the Johnstone make-up it was a suspect temperament. Jock Stein always claimed that one of his greatest achievements was to keep the fiery redhead in the game for so long. Due to this weakness, controversy dogged his career, mainly at international level, where he was never fully accepted by a section of the fans. Jimmy found this difficult to cope with and the added misfortune of injury and illness meant that his international career never reached its proper heights.

Nowadays, terms like *genius, enigma* and *legend* are too easily applied but in Johnstone's case they are appropriate. It is true to say we will probably never see his like again.

CENTENARY GLORY

The Highlight of the 80's

AS CELTIC confront the challenge of a new decade and the 1980s fade into the record books, club and fans alike can reflect on one particularly glorious achievement over 10 years sprinkled with enough success to soften the blow of the inevitable disappointments. Season 1987/88 was Celtic's *Centenary Season* and fittingly, the end of the campaign saw the club proudly crowned *League and Cup Double* winners for the eleventh time.

In retrospect, there was a certain inevitability about this Centenary Double, for surely the football gods would not allow such a historic milestone as Celtic's 100th birthday to go unmarked by substantial success. Yet at the outset, the omens were not good, despite the euphoria surrounding the return of Billy McNeill as manager in the wake of the disastrous slump of 1986/87.

In a pre-season friendly, Celtic were humbled 5-1 by Arsenal, despite McNeill's summer reconstruction, which saw the departure of several key players and the arrival of striker Andy Walker from Motherwell, full-back Chris Morris from Sheffield Wednesday and Aberdeen's experienced midfielder Billy Stark. This Arsenal reverse was aggravated by a single-goal defeat at the hands of Kenny Dalglish's Liverpool in the Tommy Burns

testimonial.

Sweet compensation came in the form of a 1-0 victory over rampant Rangers in the season's first *Old Firm* league meeting, but September saw Celtic's exit from both the League Cup and the UEFA Cup. These failures highlighted the need to strengthen the attack, a need which was met by the signings of Frank McAvennie from West Ham and Joe Miller from Aberdeen . . . and the final seeds of glory were sown.

Although by early October Celtic had slipped to third place in the league behind Aberdeen and Hearts, from that point on the season was a story of almost continuous success. By late November, top spot had been achieved following the 1-0 away defeat of Hibs — and a 2-0 win at Ibrox on 2nd January sparked genuine hopes of the title.

A nostalgic interlude in the midst of this hectic league campaign came when Kenny Dalglish, by then manager of Liverpool, made a substitute appearance in Davie Provan's testimonial match against Nottingham Forest on 30th November. It was a typically touching moment, in keeping with Celtic's fairytale tradition and hugely appreciated by the 42,000 crowd.

A thirty-one game unbeaten run ended with a 2-1 defeat at Tynecastle on 16th April. This

Hearts' victory simply did Celtic the favour of allowing them to tie up the title in front of a capacity crowd at Celtic Park the following Saturday in a 3-0 triumph over Dundee which clinched the first leg of the Centenary Double and was hailed by a chorus of *Happy Birthday to Celtic* from the delirious fans.

Undoubtedly, though, the decisive match in the campaign had been the epic 2-1 triumph at Ibrox on 20th March. Televised live, Celtic stunned everyone by going all out for victory when the pundits were predicting caution in pursuit of the draw which would consolidate their lead in the championship race. The rich reward for a positive approach was an unassailable six-point lead at the top of the table and a fairly comfortable run-in to the coveted title.

THE SCOTTISH CUP now beckoned — and the elusive dream which had seemed so improbable in the darkest days of the previous year.

Like the season itself, the early stages of the cup were uninspiring. An embarrassing replay against lowly Stranraer was only narrowly avoided courtesy of a missed penalty in a 1-0 Celtic Park victory; and it took a Billy Stark goal to squeeze through at Easter Road after a goalless home draw.

The quarter-final hurdle saw some improvement as goals from Walker, Burns and Stark at a packed Firhill saw off Partick Thistle and set up what proved to be an astonishing semi-final against Hearts. Surely this was one of the most dramatic clashes ever, with a truly stunning finale.

Trailing 1-0 in the dying minutes, Celtic dredged up all the pride and determination of their renowned cup-fighting tradition to storm the Hearts' goal in a final onslaught. Almost unbelievably, when all seemed lost, Mark McGhee and Andy Walker found the net to shatter the Edinburgh hopefuls and thrust Celtic closer to their destiny.

Cup Final Day, Saturday 14th May 1988, was the stuff of dreams. The Celtic faithful basked in glorious Hampden sunshine, perhaps lulled into a false sense of security by the carnival atmosphere as their favourites took the field. It was all too easy to ignore the threat of fellow-finalists, Dundee United, who had often proved dangerous opponents in the past — and would again that day!

Early in the second half, reality dawned when United took the lead through a devastating burst by Kevin Gallacher. Suddenly, Celtic were struggling, seemingly incapable of mounting the come-back everyone expected — and the dream was fading fast.

Enter 'Caesar', with a masterly double substitution which introduced McGhee and Stark and turned the game around. Firstly, Frank McAvennie headed the equalizer from a Rogan cross, greatly to the relief of an agonised Celtic support, by then quite happy to settle for extra time . . . but this was not a day for delaying the course of history!

With practically the last attack of the game, McAvennie somehow squeezed the ball home through a gap in United's defence . . . and suddenly it was all over. The final whistle signalled the end of an unforgettable match, brought down the curtain on a hundred magical years and became a fanfare for a glorious Centenary Double.

PAT CRERAND

IT is a sad fact that several outstanding Celtic talents never truly fulfilled their potential while wearing the hoops and Pat Crerand is a perfect example. The frustration at this fact is deepened by Pat's lifelong devotion to the club.

Gorbals-born Crerand developed his Celtic obsession while very young, becoming a regular attender at Celtic Park to watch his heroes. Before long though, his own football prowess brought him to the attention of Parkhead officials and he signed in 1957 from junior side Duntocher Hibs — at that time a productive Celtic breeding ground.

Under the guidance of the newly-appointed reserve team coach, Jock Stein, Crerand joined a reserve side which was winning trophies for the first time in 20 years. His rapid progress saw him soon stepping up to the first team, in which he made his debut against Queen of the South in October 1958.

Although the maturity of his early outings earned him a few more first team games that season, it was not until 1960-61 that he became fully established as a first-choice wing-half. By then his superb vision and intelligence were beginning to combine fully with the precision passing which was the Crerand trademark.

In spite of Pat's inspirational play, Celtic were winning nothing, although they came tantalisingly close on two occassions, losing in the Scottish Cup Final two years in a row. First, in 1961, against Dunfermline — a match which was lost 2-0 despite almost total Celtic control. For Crerand, that result was and remains, a gnawing frustration, made worse the following season, which finished on a deeply depressing note with a 3-0 drubbing by old rivals Rangers in a replayed Final.

Around that time, Pat's relations with the club hierarchy were becoming strained due to some on-field indiscipline which affected his prospects at both club and national level. It was, sadly, the beginning of the end.

Things came to a head in a dressing-room bust-up during the Old Firm New Year fixture of 1963, which Celtic lost 4-0. Crerand's simmering frustrations at the tactics being employed exploded into a raging argument, after which the talented wing-half never performed in his beloved hoops again.

A month later, he was on his way to Manchester United for a fee of £56,000. There he went on to

win league and cup honours, also emulating the feat of his former team-mates when he was a key figure in United's European Cup triumph of 1968.

The sad irony is that if things had turned out differently at Celtic Park, Pat Crerand might well have savoured the historic Lisbon glory of 1967, which would surely have fulfilled his boyhood dreams.

BILLY McNEILL

From the Manager's Chair

LAST SEASON was frankly, a major disappointment, but it is perhaps best viewed as a transitional period. We had a lot of new players in the side at the start of the season and approached the campaign optimistically. However, things began to go wrong almost from the outset.

We suffered initially — just as we had done with Mick McCarthy at the start of the 1987/88 season — in that our newly-signed centre-half, Paul Elliott, was unable to play through injury. It was only in the latter part of the season that he came to prominence.

Paul had further problems adjusting to the pace of the Scottish game but would surely have coped better had he been in from the start. This difficulty in adjusting to the pace of play created problems with referees, though I have to be honest and say that I felt Paul was unfortunate in the treatment he received from some officials. His name tended to go into the referee's notebook for an offence from which others would wander away unpunished.

Our main problem, though, was in bedding players in, a situation which prevailed throughout the season. At times it looked as though we had got things right to a large degree but we could never keep it together and produce a string of satisfactory results.

Individually, players suffered from a loss of confidence because results were not coming. We could not get on top of that lack of self-belief.

We also lost two very important players during the course of the season and the impact of that cannot be under-estimated.

My feelings on the Roy Aitken situation are well-known. It distressed me that influences outside this club were the prime reason for his insistence on leaving. Nevertheless, I was disappointed that he took it upon himself to force the situation rather than wait until the season was completed. Roy's personality and enthusiastic leadership were clearly missed at a crucial point in the season.

Tommy Burns found it difficult to reconcile himself to being at Celtic Park in a jobbing position and I could understand that. He felt that, at a fairly late stage in his career, he needed to be playing games on a regular basis. Had he been ready to turn himself to something entirely different, he had the option of remaining with

Celtic for as long as he wished.

However, he wanted to continue playing and his present position with Kilmarnock is one which will stand him in good stead for the future. I have no doubt that he will venture into coaching and management. The steps that he is taking now are very important and I feel that they will eventually enable him to return to Celtic Park in another capacity in the future.

The Roy Aitken and Tommy Burns situation rolled into one, whereby 30 years of experience at Celtic Park was lost to the rest of the team inside the space of one month, was a major blow to our prospects.

When Tommy departed, I felt that I could persuade Roy to remain with us until the end of the season. If I'd had a crystal ball, then Tommy would certainly not have been allowed to leave. As it was we simultaneously lost two players steeped in the club tradition.

We introduced the two Polish lads during the course of the season.

Jacki Dziekanowski gave us indications of his great ability early on but found it difficult to cope with the weekly demands of our game as the season developed. The physical pressures and sheer volume of games in Scotland are much greater than anything he had previously experienced. In addition, he went straight into our pre-season training from finishing the Polish League programme, so he did not have the benefit of a close-season break.

The fortunes of John Hewitt were another indication of the sort of season we experienced. He was delighted to come from Aberdeen but picked up an injury before he had a chance to show the fans his true form. X-rays showed nothing initially but eventually a detached ligament in his left knee was revealed and it was understandable that he had been inhibited dramatically.

The surgeon likened the problem to driving a Formula One car with a flat tyre. John had a remedial operation towards the end of last season and we must now hope that he will be able to show his best form in the present campaign.

Other signings found it difficult to settle in at a major club, where the demands are much greater than anything they had previously experienced. This illustrates the extent to which the buying of players is a high-risk business. You simply cannot tell how they will react to joining a club as big as Celtic.

With that in mind, I feel it is an advantage to buy from another big club as we have done in bringing Martin Hayes from Arsenal. The player has therefore been brought up with the demands of a major club and should not have as much trouble adapting to those at Celtic Park.

Likewise, other 'new' signing, Charlie Nicholas, has the benefit of big club experience with Arsenal, Aberdeen and most of all in his previous Celtic period. Obviously we are all looking to Charlie to rekindle the old magic and bring a new dimension to the club.

Great things are also expected of John Collins, signed from Hibernian during the summer. John is highly-gifted, a natural playmaker in the traditional Celtic mould, whose passing ability complements the superb skills of Paul McStay in an exciting new midfield combination.

I have indicated that the fact of starting the '89/'90 campaign with so many new players contributed to our problems but I believe that to be something to which we must adjust.

Freedom-of-contract means that players now have the opportunity to seek big money when their contracts are up and all clubs have to accept this new scenario, for better or worse.

LOOKING BACK on key moments in the course of the season, the emotional impact of the Partizan Belgrade game at Celtic Park was quite remarkable. The game itself was one of the most dramatic in which I have ever been involved. We made mistakes, put them behind us in the best possible way (by scoring goals) and had the tie all-but-won until we conceded a goal in the final moments. The outcome hit the players heavily and I would love to know the sort of impetus victory in such a game might have given us. We won some games immediately after the match but they were hard-working results rather than victories achieved by inspired play.

We went off the boil again before stringing together a good run up to Christmas. The team was playing well but went to Tynecastle and dropped a point in a poor game. There were chances to win, including a penalty kick, and the manner in which we failed was a setback.

Then, in the final game of 1989, we were beaten 2-0 at home by Dunfermline Athletic in another game which we dominated. Again a missed penalty kick cost us dearly.

Emotionally and psychologically, we suffered blows at the wrong time and those Festive Season reverses ran together with the sorry Roy Aitken transfer saga. After that we began to struggle quite dramatically.

I HAVE NO DOUBT that our players were a great deal better than our results suggested but that is no excuse for what went wrong. Our major failing during the course of the season was in the goal-scoring department. At the end of the day, that failure was our downfall.

We had problems elsewhere but, for the most part, the defence and midfield performed as we would have anticipated.

THERE WERE PLUSSES to be taken from the season also. 'Packy' Bonner displayed the sort of form which we have come to expect of him. Goalkeepers tend to respond favourably when required to do that bit more and we know that he is a superb man to have at the back.

Dariusz Wdowczyk gave indications that he, too, can be a superb player for us. He helped to give the defence a look of stability and we can reasonably expect better still from him in the season ahead when he has a clearer picture of Scottish football and is that much more settled in Scotland.

The centre-back combination of Paul Elliott and Derek Whyte also looked towards the end of the season as if it could be a very satisfactory one for us. People tend to forget that Derek is still in his early twenties and has plenty of learning in front of him. Danny McGrain, who became one of the best defenders in the world, only made his début for Celtic at the age of 21, whereas Derek has already chalked up nearly 200 appearances for the club.

It was also encouraging to see emerging talent at the club once more in the persons of such as Steve Fulton and Gerry Creaney. They were brought into the first team set-up on occasions and gave clear indication of their ability, though they still have a lot of work in front of them.

Football is a hard profession for youngsters. Those with ability must appreciate the heavy demands of continued progress. Only those with the right attitude get on in this game.

WE HAVE WORKED very hard in the development of our own players at Celtic Park. Benny Rooney was brought in to contribute in that direction and it is an area in which we will invest still more heavily in the years ahead.

Our ambition is to re-establish the nursery system which provided the club with so many outstanding players in the past and we have some who have begun to give an indication that they can be great players for the club in the future.

You can only bring youngsters into the first team for short periods at any given time and must nurse them carefully. Ideally, they should be brought in, given experience and then left out again with relatively few demands made of them.

In any case, I do not think that 18 or 19-year-olds are the answer to the demands of the Premier Division. An extended apprenticeship, such as served by Danny McGrain, would give a player a greater chance of breaking through in the top team but, nowadays, the attitude seems to be that if you have not broken through by the time you are 20, you have had it.

DESPITE all the difficulties, it is my firm intention to ensure that Celtic make a strong challenge on all fronts in the present season. I believe that this can be done, despite the inflationary transfer market, which shows that there are not as many quality players about as there used to be.

PRIZE QUIZ

Celtic in Europe

TEST your knowledge and WIN a FABULOUS DAY at CELTIC PARK. Full V.I.P. treatment for two on a Match Day (to be arranged with lucky Winners). The Prize includes Lunch, Match Tickets and other *"extras"* — in short, a never-to-be-forgotten day out for any Celtic fan!

1. Name the seven Celts who appeared in both the Lisbon and Milan European Cup Finals.

2. What was the score in Celtic's European Cup Winners' Cup match against Ghent in October 1984?

3. Which of Celtic's two European Cup Finals attracted the biggest crowd, Lisbon or Milan?

4. Who was Celtic's goalkeeper when they defeated T.P.S. Turku in the 1973-'74 European Cup?

5. What do Celtic's European Cup matches against Ajax (1970/'71) and Rosenborg Trondheim (1972/'73) have in common?

6. How many goals did Celtic lose in the 1966-'67 European Cup?

7. Who were Celtic drawn to play before the draw was revised in the 1968-'69 European Cup?

8. Which one of Celtic's 1967 European squad had previously appeared in a European Final?

9. Which unique feat did Celtic achieve when ousting Leeds from the 1969-'70 European Cup?

10. How many times have Celtic been defeated in the first round of the European Cup, by whom and in which years?

WELCOME HOME *Charlie*

VERY FEW professional footballers substituted in a competitive game receive a standing ovation from the *opposition* supporters as they leave the field of play.

The fact that Charlie Nicholas should enjoy such a reception at Celtic Park while representing great rivals Aberdeen says a lot for the level of affection he earned during his all-too-brief spell with his first league club.

And when Charlie finally completed the move back to Celtic seven years after leaving for Arsenal, it was obvious that the affection truly was a two-way affair.

"Celtic was the only club I was really interested in joining," he stated. "I had great times with the club early in my career under the same manager and it was a marvellous feeling to be going back."

Not *all* Celtic fans remained faithful to Nicholas when he moved on in 1983. He came in for considerable 'stick' on his first appearance at Celtic Park in an Arsenal jersey and a few, apparently, could never reconcile themselves to his departure.

But, in numbers which increased with each appearance against the club closest to his heart, Celtic supporters simply could not find it in them to sever the strong bond they had with the player years earlier.

The reconciliation culminated in that extraordinary standing ovation and repeated chorus of his name when he walked off Celtic Park 20 minutes from the end of a vital clash between Celtic and Aberdeen on December 2nd 1989.

The uncharitable could point out that Celtic were leading 1-0 and that the reception for Nicholas might have been just a little different had the opposite been the case. Perhaps so, but it will remain in the memories of most of those present for a long time.

Not surprisingly, the reaction of some Aberdeen supporters to the whole event was less enthusiastic but Nicholas remained the complete professional.

He never hid his affection for Celtic — but he never gave less than 100% effort against them.

Charlie is a completely different player to the one who left Celtic Park seven years ago but the prospect of his popularity being diminished is remote.

His summer signing after weeks of rumour and speculation was a cause of celebration for many. His influence will surely lead to several more in the months ahead. He is back where he belongs.

Welcome home, Charlie!

Charlie and his lovely wife Claire

JIMMY McGRORY

JIMMY McGRORY was, quite simply, the greatest goalscorer in the history of Scottish Football and grew into a Celtic legend between the two World Wars. He was the ideal club player, hard but always fair, a true gentleman of the game and a prolific scorer.

As well as his playing exploits, McGrory made a significant contribution on the administration side, both as Manager in the post-World War II period and later as Public Relations Officer. But it was as a player that he excelled, establishing a record of 550 goals at a rate of more than one per game — a target unlikely ever to be equalled in the Scottish game.

One of a family of seven, living in Garngad, McGrory's mother died while the children were still young and he lost his father soon after joining Celtic in 1922. The club became his new family and he more or less dedicated his life to it.

Following occasional first-team outings, he was loaned out to Clydebank for the 1923-24 season, which was to prove a disastrous one for Celtic. McGrory was recalled to Celtic Park after scoring there for Clydebank. From then on the goals flowed and such was his legendary power in the air, that at least a third of his massive total were scored with the head.

McGrory's dedication to the club was total. Shortly after his world-record goalscoring feat of eight against Dunfermline Athletic in January 1928, he rejected the mighty Arsenal's approaches in favour of his beloved Celtic.

Though deeply affected by the tragic death of his great friend John Thomson, Jimmy battled on with great distinction throughout the 1930's. One of his most famous goals, reputed to have given birth to the famous Hampden Roar, came for Scotland against England in 1933. However, perhaps surprisingly, his international career was a modest one, with only seven caps and he never appeared at Wembley.

McGrory's playing career was ended by injury against Queen's Park on 16th October 1937. Typically, he scored in the game — a goal which was to be his last, as during the lay-off he accepted an offer to manage Kilmarnock.

Returning to Celtic Park as Manager in 1945, the McGrory record was undistinguished apart from notable triumphs such as the Coronation Cup of 1953, the 1954 League and Cup Double and the immortal 7-1 League Cup Final defeat of Rangers in 1957. He made way for Jock Stein in 1965 and proudly witnessed his successor's fantastic achievements from his new position as P.R.O.

Jimmy McGrory died in October 1982 but to Celtic supporters who cherish tradition, he is immortal.

THE REARING of potential first-team players through Celtic Boys' Club and the youth and reserve sides has long been a feature of Celtic Football Club. Both the recent past-captain and the present skipper, Roy Aitken and Paul McStay, were Celtic Boys' Club products, as were first-team stars of the past decade Tommy Burns, George McCluskey, Charlie Nicholas, Peter Grant and Derek Whyte.

It is a record which no Scottish club can better but football supporters always prefer to look to the present and future rather than the past, so Celtic fans are impatient to know who is next in line.

The fiercely competitive nature of the Premier Division makes the blooding of talented youngsters a risky business, especially for a club as big as Celtic, which is always expected to be challenging for honours. Still, the good news is that the present crop of reserve team players appears to comprise as wide-ranging a display of gifted and eager youngsters as any in the past 10 years.

Closest to making a real break-through last season was left-sided midfielder *Steve Fulton*, who started 16 first team games and always impressed as a player able to pass the ball accurately and retain possession comfortably. Twenty years old in August, Fulton will see the present season as the one in which he must begin to command a regular place in the top team and continue to develop his game.

He has the talent to play effectively in any left-sided role, though his future seems sure to be in midfield and his ability certainly excites manager Billy McNeill. The boss has gone on record as saying that Fulton is the best passer of a ball at the club and clearly believes that the youngster can become one of the genuine stars of the Scottish game in the final decade of the 20th century.

Prolific goal-scoring form for the reserve sides after the turn of the year brought 20-year-old striker *Gerry Creaney* into the Celtic Park limelight and he too was given a first team chance towards the end of the season. The

YOUTH
The Hope for the Future

Steve Fulton

circumstances says a lot for his ability and confident outlook.

Gerry has been compared with an earlier Celtic Boys' Club product, George McCluskey, in terms of style and he accepts it as a compliment because "George had a tremendous amount of skill." But he adds cheekily: "I would like to think that I work a little harder off the ball!"

Creaney is another youngster of whom boss Billy McNeill has high hopes, though he stressed the importance of being able to introduce such players into a winning first-team set-up. That is something he hopes to be in a position to do this season.

Creaney's striking partner in the reserves for much of last season, *Dugald McCarrison*, is another product of the club's youth policy who could force his way into first-team reckoning this season.

highlight of that goal-scoring sequence was a four-goal blast against a Hearts side which featured ex-Celt Brian Whittaker as his direct opponent and former Ranger Nicky Walker in goal.

Creaney also found himself lining up against Motherwell's first-team captain and Scotland 'B' internationalist Tom Boyd in a reserve match and Aberdeen's Willie Miller, who needs no introductions, in another. On each occasion, though, the young Celt took on his direct opponent before firing spectacular goals past the respective keepers, Alistair Maxwell and reigning Scottish P.F.A. *Player of the Year*, Theo Snelders.

His success against top quality opposition persuaded Billy McNeill that the confident youngster could be fielded at top-team level without worries over his ability to cope.

Creaney started two of the final seven Premier Division games of the season and came on as substitute in four more, opening his first-team goals account with a dramatic late equaliser in a home match against Dundee, when Celtic were down to ten men because of an injury to Paul Elliott.

He did not appear in a winning team, though, as Celtic finished their league campaign with a dismal run of results. That he should create a favourable impression in such difficult

Dugald McCarrison

Twenty-one three days before Christmas, McCarrison actually made his first-team debut as a 17-year-old in the early months of Celtic's fantastic Double-winning Centenary Year. The occasion was not an auspicious one as the team suffered its only home defeat of the campaign, a 2-1 loss to Dundee United, but the youngster showed abundant promise. He returned to the first-team frame late in the 1988-89 season and made a real impact by scoring a fine headed goal in his appearance as substitute against Dundee at Dens Park.

However, last season brought no further top-team involvement and the youngster could well have accepted defeat and sought a move. Instead, he knuckled down, battled through a lean spell early in the reserve programme and finished on a real high. He scored eight goals in his final six reserve-team matches, including the only goal of the Reserve League Cup final against Dundee at Dens Park and gave notice that he was again pushing strongly for a first-team chance.

It was a push noted by manager Billy McNeill who indicated, as he reviewed the end of the season, that McCarrison could well feature at the start of the new campaign.

David Elliot

Pacey midfielder *David Elliot*, who started two games and made two appearances as substitute the previous season, suffered a mid-season set-back through injury but was twice included in the first-team pool later in the campaign and made substitute appearances on both occasions. They were unfortunate matches in which to be involved — Celtic suffered home defeats at the hands of Motherwell (1-0) and St Mirren (3-0) — but they served notice of the fact that the explosive left-sided attacker, 21 in November, was still very much in the frame.

Nineteen-year-old right-back *Mark McNally* was an impressively consistent performer at reserve level and was only denied a first-team debut chance by a bad ankle injury collected in a reserve outing against Albion Rovers. A couple of weeks later, illness prevented Chris Morris from lining up against Motherwell at Fir Park and the manager indicated that McNally would have been given the No. 2 jersey had he been fit.

It was little consolation for the youngster, who had earlier captained the under-18 side (as one of two over-age players) to victory in the Glasgow Cup competition, but again demonstrated that he was very much in the boss's mind for a step-up when the time is right.

Right-winger *Alex Mathie*, 22 the same day as McCarrison celebrates his 21st birthday, started six first-team games and came on as substitute in another last season though he also missed part of the campaign through illness. In those half-dozen outings, he showed glimpses of the dazzling pace and directness which made him stand out in reserve games time and again but generally lacked the service required to give him a real chance of staking a claim for a permanent spot in the side.

Alex Mathie

However, his speed means that he will be a threat at any level and it could well be that he can yet make his mark at Celtic Park.

Keeper *Andy Murdoch*, 22 in July, found himself Pat Bonner's immediate deputy following the transfer of Ian Andrews to Southampton and manager McNeill professed

Andy Murdoch

viewers associate with the family name. *Gerry Britton* scored goals galore — he actually emerged as top scorer for the reserve teams, ahead of Creaney and McCarrison — and the more experienced trio of *Steve McCahill, Stuart Balmer* and *Paul McLaughlin* formed a solid defensive base for the side.

Further down the ladder, stars of Scotland's magnificent World Youth Cup campaign, *Billy Dolan, Jim Beattie* and *Brian O'Neil* showed precocious talent in abundance for the Reserve League West side and the youth team.

They, along with right-winger *Sean McBride*, will surely push further along the path towards eventual first-team appearances by forcing their way into the Premier Reserve League set-up.

In addition, fans may rest assured that there are many gifted teenagers currently starring for Celtic Boys' Club ready to make the step up to youth team football in the near future.

Steve McCahill

himself quite happy to have the youngster, signed from Johnstone Burgh, as the club's No. 2 keeper.

Murdoch gained much valuable experience during the season in loan spells with First Division clubs Partick Thistle and Hamilton Academical. In each case, the loan was sought by John Lambie, whose moves from Thistle to Hamilton and back again made several headlines during the season, and the man in question made no effort to disguise the esteem in which he held the young keeper.

Indeed, Lambie confidently predicted that Murdoch was a Scottish internationalist in the making, an evaluation made to look possible by some superb displays from the Greenock-born keeper.

Dubliner *Declan Roche*, who turned 20 in October, made genuine progress during last season and was very much a vital part of the side which won the Reserve League Cup and finished the Premier Reserve League with an unbeaten nine-game run which carried Celtic to second spot.

Recognition of the advances made came with a call-up for the Republic of Ireland's under-21 international against Malta in April, a game in which Declan made a worthwhile contribution in an unfamiliar right-midfield role.

Raymond McStay, younger brother of club captain Paul, showed many of the skills which

WELCOME ABOARD

Bhoys!

New Signings

MARTIN HAYES

MARTIN HAYES was Arsenal's top scorer in the 1986-87 season with 24 competitive goals, 12 of them penalty kicks, when he held down a regular place in attack alongside Niall Quinn and Charlie Nicholas. Was used mainly wide on the left but, being naturally right-sided, prefers performing on the right of midfield and hopes to be playing in that position with Celtic. Started 92 games for the *Gunners* in five seasons in the first team pool and appeared as substitute in 40 more, scoring a total of 34 goals. Has three England under-21 caps.

JOHN COLLINS

A PRODUCT of Celtic Boys' Club, John Collins has matured into one of the most gifted players in the country. The Scotland international midfielder opted to join Celtic in preference to a pack of continental clubs who had been tracking him since he went out-of-contract at Hibs. John is a young man with the world at his feet and it's great to still have him in Scotland — especially at Celtic Park!

25

TOMMY BURNS

A Tribute to a Great Celt

THERE IS SOMETHING essentially Celtic about Tommy Burns. He is liked by most of the support, adored by a few and widely respected by opponents. When he went to Kilmarnock in December 1989, it was hard to envisage him in the alien blue of another side, so accustomed were we to associating him with Celtic.

Even today he is far more likely to be referred to as *Tommy Burns, ex-Celt*, than *Tommy Burns of Kilmarnock*. This in spite of the significant part he played in helping the Ayrshire outfit gain promotion to the First Division of the Scottish League!

He was born in 1956, and joined Celtic from Maryhill Juniors in 1975. Jock Stein had spotted something special in this redhead and, by the spring of that year, he made his first appearance as a substitute in a game against Dundee at Parkhead.

The league had been well lost by that time and in truth, the club was at the crossroads. Rangers had at last ended the run of 9 League Championships in a row, Billy McNeill was on the point of announcing his retirement and it cannot have been the most settled of times for a youngster to make his debut.

In the summer, Jock Stein suffered his horrendous road accident and was out of action for more or less all of the following season. For Tommy, it was back to the reserves until he got a late run in the team as the championship challenge was fading.

He did have one outstanding game in the midfield in a 0-0 draw against Rangers at Parkhead, when discerning spectators consoled themselves over the loss of the league (and everything else that season) by the thought that this youngster with the flaming red hair might be one for the future.

The following season (1976-77), Tommy really began to make his mark. It was a strange season. Although the championship was won back, the team rarely had a settled look about it and Tommy, for all his precocious brilliance, was never consistent enough to command a permanent place.

Early in the season, Celtic lost at Tannadice. It was a poor display, with Dalglish looking strangely out of sorts, but again that striking red hair (more noticeable in those long-haired days of the mid-seventies) caught the eye, as did the accompanying ball skills and distribution.

Later that autumn Tommy had a galling experience when an outplayed Aberdeen team won the League Cup. This had been his first Hampden occasion and although he was substituted by the veteran Bobby Lennox, he did not disgrace himself.

In the league campaign, he appeared 22 times (counting substitutions) and was on the bench for the Cup Final victory over Rangers. The youngster was earning his spurs!

The Celtic team of 1977 was dangerously over-reliant on Kenny Dalglish but in August of that year he moved to Liverpool amidst weeping and gnashing of teeth. Much was expected of Tommy in taking over the role of playmaker at Celtic Park but sadly, it was asking too much at that time.

The following season saw the return of Billy McNeill and the triumphant recapturing of the championship; but questions were beginning to be asked about Burns. McNeill had bought well in Murdo MacLeod and Davie Provan and Burns was very prone to off-days and injuries. He displayed a tendency at times to slow the game down when the opposite was clearly required. Nevertheless, he did play 28 games in the Premier Division, although he was missing from the 4-2 epic which won the championship.

Tommy won his first Scottish Cup medal the following year in the 1-0 victory over Rangers, then played in almost every game the next season when the Premier Division was won in fine style.

The title was secured at Tannadice in April, and Tommy scored the third goal from a long way out. It was a fitting end to the league campaign, for Celtic had had a fine run since the New Year with Burns outstanding in almost every game. It was now clear that the brilliant redhead had learned to blend his undoubted talent with consistency.

Such performances brought him the first of only a handful of international honours. Tommy is not the only Celt whom many believe to have been badly treated by international selectors and I am convinced he would have been a huge success in the 1982 World Cup Finals in Spain, where his style of play would surely have suited the balmy nights in Malaga and Seville.

Another league title came Celtic's way in 1982, and the League Cup the following December; but 1983 and the following years were difficult ones for the club. Frequently, Tommy would show his brilliance but all-too-often the general poor performances of the team dragged him down as well and he frequently gave the impression of being listless, moody and unsettled.

When he did turn it on, however, it was a sight to behold. One such occasion was a UEFA Cup game against Sporting Lisbon. Down 2-0 from the first leg in Portugal, the large Parkhead crowd was hopeful but hardly confident about the eventual outcome. Tommy chose that night to play the best game of his career and Celtic won 5-0.

Tommy scored the first goal, then dictated the midfield like Bobby Murdoch or Peter Wilson of old and Celtic were *world class*. Unfortunately it was a false dawn but the memory of that game will linger long.

Celtic were never really in the hunt in the league in 1985, but the Cup was won. Sadly for Tommy, he was substituted in the Final and quite a lot of us must have wondered whether his green and white days were numbered. The full-time whistle, however, saw Tommy as ecstatic as any other fan and not for the first time, we saw him taking time to show the trophy to handicapped supporters, an action which spoke volumes for the man.

Tommy started off season 1985/86 at left-back of all places. While not a failure there, it was not his best position.

This was another season of severe disappointment soothed by eventual triumph in the league, when Hearts 'lost their bottle' (and the match by 2-0) at Dens Park on the last day, under pressure from transistors in the crowd which obligingly told them that Celtic were tanking St Mirren at Love Street. Burns had enjoyed a fine consistent season, especially when moved to his normal position in the middle of the field.

The less said about season 1986/87 the better but with the return of Billy McNeill as manager and several astute buys, Tommy once again came into his own in the double-winning season of 1987/88. He collected his third Cup Winner's medal in 1988 and a fourth in 1989, both thoroughly deserved.

When he moved to Kilmarnock there was sadness all round at the departure of such a fine Celt. Although now 33 and clearly finding the demands of the Premier Division too much, Tommy was unhappy about leaving the team he loved. Perhaps some day he will return to his natural home at Celtic Park to bring his wider experience and encyclopaedic knowledge of the game to bear in some capacity.

There is so much about Tommy Burns that marks him out as a gentleman of the game. He is polite and pleasant to supporters; he plays the game hard but fairly, although no stranger to yellow and even red cards. (Once at Paisley he somehow managed to get himself dismissed *after* he had been substituted!)

Nevertheless, he is hardly a discipline problem and will be a great asset to Kilmarnock for his tough, yet sensible and thoughtful approach to the game. *He is, in short, a fine professional.*

There is one incident for which I will personally remember him more than any other. It was a game at Parkhead and Tommy had, frankly, made a hash of a lovely through-ball. Instead of bawling out someone else, Tommy turned to the 'jungle', put his finger to his forehead like a revolver and "shot" himself.

It was his way of saying, "Sorry, bhoys!" It was also his way of letting the fans know that, star or not, his heart was still on the terracing with them.

What a player! What a Celt! What a man!

JOE MILLER

THE HIGHS and lows experienced by Celtic Football Club in the three full seasons since Billy McNeill returned to the position of manager reflect the fluctuating fortunes of one of his major early signings.

Diminutive forward Joe Miller, an instant favourite with supporters, has played a major part in the three glorious trophy triumphs since the summer of 1987 but sometimes his form has frustrated the fans.

His dramatic signing captured the imagination of the Celtic support and they turned out in force to see his debut against Dundee at Celtic Park. His first touches were good. Andy Walker scored twice in the opening five minutes and an impressive 5-0 victory was rounded off with a splendid goal from the debutant.

A few days later, clever wing play by Miller set up Walker's opening goal in a 2-0 win over Motherwell at Fir Park and the new signing's place in the hearts of the Celtic fans was secure.

Suddenly, Celtic were winning games in style once more and good festive season results, including a 2-1 win over Dundee United at Tannadice when Miller scored a dramatic last-minute header, put them in pole position for the championship.

The title was all but won before the newcomer even tasted defeat in a Celtic jersey, though the 2-1 league defeat by Hearts at Tynecastle was little more than a hiccup.

With the championship secured a week later, attention turned to the Scottish Cup Final against Dundee United. Despite a worrying dip in Joe's recent form and the first-half miss of a great chance, the little winger's contribution to the dramatic last-gasp victory was immense.

Joe's poor form as well as injury cost him his place for much of the following season. Then fate took a hand as Andy Walker was forced to miss out on the end of the season because of a serious eye injury and with recent signing Tommy Coyne cup-tied, Miller was fielded in the central striking role he fancied, alongside the experienced Mark McGhee.

Success came immediately as Miller scored the only goal of the game in each of Celtic's final two league games then, much more importantly, did likewise in the Scottish Cup Final against Rangers, denying the Ibrox side a coveted treble success.

Once again an end-of-season high was followed by major disappointment at the start of the following campaign, as Miller suffered another injury in pre-season training and missed out on the first six weeks of competitive action.

On his return, he was unable to hold down a regular place in the side as minor injuries and the manager's regular changes of striking personnel in search of goals took effect.

Indifferent performances were mixed with sparkling ones as the forward's form again mirrored the club's fortunes. High points included a crucial part in the goal which once more inflicted Scottish Cup agony on rivals Rangers and an amazing goal in the quarter-final replay against Dunfermline Athletic.

He conjured up another memorable individual display in his third consecutive Scottish Cup Final appearance at Hampden. On a day of heroic contributions, no-one wore his heart on his jersey more than Miller whose strength-sapping runs at the Aberdeen rearguard were a regular, though fruitless feature.

Enigmatic he may be but Joe Miller is immensely talented and is sure to one day fulfil his enormous potential, both with Celtic and Scotland. Skill such as his should make Joe a strong contender for international honours as the trail to the 1994 World Cup Finals in the United States gets underway.

Career Statistics											
Season	League		League Cup		Scottish Cup		Europe		Total	
	Apps	Goals	Apps	Goals	Apps	Goals	Apps	Goals	Apps	Goals
87-88	24(3)	3			5(1)				29(4)	3
88-89	16(6)	8	3		3	1	2		24(6)	9
89-90	16(8)	5	(1)		6	1	1		23(9)	6
Total	56(17)	16	3(1)		14(1)	2	3		76(19)	18

Numbers in brackets indicate additional appearances as substitute.

YOUTH TEAM VICTORY

Under·18 Glasgow Cup

CUP *firsts* and *one-offs* have always been a proud tradition in the 102-year history of Celtic Football Club:

* Scottish Cup Finalists at the first attempt.
* First British winners of the European Champions' Cup, again at the first attempt.
* Winners of the prestigious Empire Exhibition and Coronation Cups, both very much against the odds, in opposition to the top clubs from north and south of the border.

In this respect, the 1989-90 season, in many ways so disappointing at first-team level, saw a small but significant extension of the Celtic tradition of cup *firsts* through the success of their youngest players in the inaugural Under-18 Glasgow Cup. This was a victory made all the sweeter by its achievement with characteristic Celtic style and flair.

The new youth event grew out of the Glasgow F.A.'s long-standing knockout competition for the five senior clubs in Scotland's largest city. This old-style Glasgow Cup had become such a low-key affair in recent years that it was decided to have the impressive trophy contested by under-18 teams from the various clubs. This gave the cream of Glasgow's young talent the opportunity to exhibit their skills in one of only two professional youth competitions in the Scottish footballing calendar.

Celtic, Rangers, Partick Thistle, Clyde and Queen's Park all played each other once in group competition, with the top two going on to contest the final.

Very disappointed at losing out to Clydebank in the first round of their defence of the national B.P. Youth Cup, the Celtic youngsters seized the opportunity, playing some highly-entertaining, attacking football which delighted the sizeable crowds. They began their campaign on a chilly November day with a match against Clyde at Shettleston. After a nervous start, a satisfactory 3-1 win was recorded with two goals from Gary Bendoris and a late clincher from Gerry Britton.

A week later the outcome was the same — another comfortable 3-1 victory for the young Celts over their Queen's Park counterparts.

Winger Sean McBride opened the scoring and after a Queen's equaliser, the deadly Britton took his tournament tally to three with two strikes midway through the second half.

The next clash was predictably billed as the *final before the final* when firm qualifying favourites, Celtic and Rangers, met at

Shettleston. A niggly match ended in triumph for Celtic's cup-fighting qualities as their gritty determination earned a 1-0 victory, playing the entire second half with 10 men following the dismissal of left-back Kenny Campbell for a second bookable offence. The depleted Celtic side survived a period of intense Rangers pressure before fighting back to score a late winner through substitute Steve Dornan.

Buoyed by a win which secured their place in the final, Celtic completed their qualifying programme by going to town on luckless Partick Thistle, who suffered a 7-2 drubbing. Inevitably, Britton notched two of the goals, the other marksmen being Campbell, Brian O'Neil, McBride, Kevin Finnon and Chris Rough as Celtic swarmed around the Thistle goal in the second half.

So Celtic topped the qualifying group with a 100% record, scoring 14 goals for the loss of just 4 and in the process recording the biggest win of the tournament. Their opponents in the final would be Rangers, who came from behind to defeat Clyde 4-3 in their last qualifying match to secure second spot and set up yet another Old Firm cup decider.

Fittingly, Celtic saved their most mature performance for the Hampden showdown, played in front of a crowd of 6,500 on Hogmanay afternoon. There were no failures in a fine team performance, highlighted by the outstanding individual displays of captain Mark McNally and Jim Beattie in central defence, right-back Billy Dolan and winger McBride.

That man Britton opened the scoring just before half-time, his sixth strike of the competition. The Celts attacked relentlessly after the interval, with McBride in dazzling form. Eventually, Bendoris scored a second, effectively clinching a victory which could have been more emphatic if Celtic had cashed in on further chances.

In any case, the 2-0 scoreline was comprehensive enough to confirm the young Celts as Glasgow's best youth side and gave the thousands of fans who witnessed the stylish performance an appetising glimpse of the future.

1965

...that was the year that was

... "There's a New World somewhere,
They call the Promised Land" ...

THIS WAS the opening line of the No. 1 song in the pop charts on March 9th, 1965 — and how prophetic these words now seem to Celtic supporters, for that was the day Jock Stein returned to Celtic as manager. Mr Stein's move from Hibernian to Celtic had been announced at a Parkhead Press Conference on January 31st: Stein would stay with Hibs "until a replacement had been found." By March, Bob Shankly, brother of Liverpool's Bill, had been lured to Easter Road from Dens Park where he had led Dundee to the League Championship in 1962. Jock Stein's last game in charge of Hibs was a Scottish Cup quarter-final against Rangers at Easter Road on March 3rd. Hibs won 2-1, their third victory over Rangers that season, despite the surprise return to the Rangers team of Jim Baxter — his first game for three months following a broken leg injury.

The Celtic which Jock Stein inherited was in disarray. The club had failed to win a major domestic trophy since beating Rangers 7-1 in the 1957-58 League Cup Final; promising players like Bobby Carroll, John Colrain and Mike McVittie had failed to fulfil their potential. Others, like John Divers, John Hughes, Steve Chalmers and Charlie Gallagher were first team mainstays who lacked direction. Jimmy Johnstone and Bobby Murdoch were the brightest hopes for the future, Bobby Lennox appeared to be destined for mediocrity, and Billy McNeill, the captain of Celtic and Scotland, was in danger of stagnating if he stayed with the Celts much longer.

Celtic had slumped so badly in the winter of 1964-65 that, following the inevitable Ne'er Day defeat at Ibrox (by 1-0, with Murdoch missing a penalty and Johnstone being sent off), journalist John Fairgrieve was moved to comment about the club:—

... "They are being left behind by provincial clubs with a fraction of their resources. They are being left so far behind by Rangers that it is no longer a race." (Scottish Daily Mail, 12th January 1965).

A run of heavy league defeats was brought to an end with a stunning display against Aberdeen

on January 30th at Celtic Park. The players, perhaps sensing a wind of change, scorched to an 8-0 victory, with John 'Yogi' Hughes, revelling in the icy conditions in his rubber-soled boots, scoring five. Murdoch, Auld and Lennox completed the rout. Twenty-four hours later came the bombshell news of Jock Stein's imminent arrival, and six weeks later, Bob Kelly the Celtic Chairman, greeted his returning protégé 'with a firm handshake and the words "It's all yours now" ...' (Campbell, Tom & Woods, Pat, *The Glory and the Dream*, Mainstream Publishing, Edinburgh, 1986).

The news of Stein's appointment had an immediate, galvanising effect upon the players. They followed up the blitzing of Aberdeen with a convincing 3-0 win over St Mirren at Love Street in the Scottish Cup 1st round and repeated the treatment in the league the following week by 5-1. Then after scraping through nervously by a Lennox goal against Queen's Park in the Scottish Cup 2nd round at

Jock Stein and Jimmy McGrory

Skipper Billy McNeill and the victorious Scottish Cup Team of 1965

Hampden, they dealt successive league and cup defeats at Celtic Park to the champions-elect, Kilmarnock, by 2-0 and 3-2 respectively.

Jock Stein's first game in charge was against Airdrie at Broomfield on Wednesday, 10th March, and Bertie Auld took the opportunity to impress his new boss, scoring five goals in Celtic's 6-0 win. John Hughes got the other goal.

The bubble burst with a 0-1 defeat v. St Johnstone the following Saturday, after which the story of season '64-'65 was one of stuttering league form and smooth progress in the cup. Motherwell gave Celtic a fright in the semi-final at Hampden, drawing the first game 2-2 before going down 3-0 in a replay.

The Scottish Cup Final of 1965, Celtic v. Dunfermline Athletic on April 24th, was the game which, by common consent, marked the beginning of the Stein era at Celtic Park. The notorious 'Hampden Swirl' played a part in an absorbing final. Dunfermline, playing into the blustery wind, took the lead in 15 minutes when Fallon was tempted too far out of his goal and could only fingertip the ball as far as Dunfermline captain Harry Melrose, who smartly hooked it into the empty net. Celtic equalised in 31 minutes. A great drive from Gallagher struck the crossbar, soared high into the air and was blown down and back into play by the wind. The alert Bertie Auld had stationed himself underneath the dropping ball and he outjumped the Fife defence to head home.

Dunfermline snatched an opportunist goal one minute before half time, McLaughlin scoring with a low, angled drive from Melrose's tapped free kick. Such a blow would have knocked the stuffing out of the pre-Stein Celtic but not this

team. They set about Dunfermline in the second half, forcing them onto the defensive. Auld and Lennox sliced open the *Pars'* defence with a series of one-twos which culminated in Auld boring deep into the box before carefully driving home his and Celtic's second equaliser in the 51st minute. From then on, wave after wave of green and white attacks broke upon the solid black and white defensive wall, until Bobby Lennox forced a historic corner kick on the Celtic left. It was nine minutes from time, at the Mount Florida end. Charlie Gallagher flighted the ball perfectly for Billy McNeill to soar in and head Celtic's winner.

It was a moment of destiny for McNeill and for Celtic. As Tom Campbell describes it:—

... "For perhaps two seconds, Hampden's vast bowl was still, stunned by the sudden shock of decision and then erupted into bedlam. The roar continued, minute after minute and its prevailing note changed: it was not a roar of joy that a Cup Final produces; rather, it was a tumultuous welcome to the future and the instinctive realization by all Celtic's support that the young men had grown up and that nothing, now or in the years to come, would withstand the collective spirit of their manhood." (Tom Campbell, *Glasgow Celtic 1945-70*, Civic Press, Glasgow 1970).

Jock Stein himself acknowledged the significance of this win years later when he reflected that, "It would not have gone so well for Celtic had they not won this game." The Celtic team that day was: Fallon; Young & Gemmell; Murdoch, McNeill & Clark; Chalmers & Gallagher; Hughes; Lennox and Auld.

The summer of 1965 was long, hot and pleasurable for Celtic fans. At last, Rangers had been outgunned in terms of trophy-winning: Kilmarnock pipped Hearts to the League Title by 0.04 of a goal (in the days of *goal average*) by winning 2-0 at Tynecastle while Celtic were winning the Cup at Hampden and the 'Gers had to be content with the League Cup.

Jock Stein agreed to take charge of the Scottish national team for the duration of the 1966 World Cup qualifying matches, following the parting of the previous boss Ian McColl and led the team to a creditable 1-1 draw with Poland in Chorzow on May 23rd and a competent 2-1 win over Finland in Helsinki four days later.

Stein made one significant close-season signing on June 5th, taking Joe McBride from Motherwell for £22,500. Meanwhile, the supporters went off on holiday, anticipating the new season with relish. That summer they watched Peter Thomson of Australia win his fifth and last British Open Golf Championship at Royal Birkdale and another Australian, Roy Emerson, win his second consecutive Wimbledon Singles Title, beating his countryman Fred Stolle in the final — Stolle's third consecutive final defeat. Yet another Aussie — the awesome Margaret Smith (later Mrs Barry Court) — took the Ladies' Title by beating the graceful Brazilian, Maria Bueno. Scotland's Jim Clark won the British Grand Prix in a Lotus-Climax, en route to his second World Drivers' Championship. Elvis Presley's *Crying in the Chapel*, the Hollies' *I'm Alive* and the Byrds' *Mr Tambourine Man* took turns at the No. 1 chart position. In the cinema, Peter O'Toole starred in *Lawrence of Arabia* and the Beatles' film *Help!* was a huge success. The title song naturally shot to No. 1 . . . then it was back to football business.

All the high expectations seemed to be justified when English First Division side Sunderland,

Jim Baxter and all, were dismantled 5-0 on their own Roker Park pitch. A couple of hiccups followed in the League Cup sectional games for 1965-66. Dundee United beat Celtic 2-1 at Tannadice in the first competitive game of the new season. Motherwell were narrowly beaten 1-0 at Parkhead the following Wednesday, then Dundee came to Celtic Park, defended in depth and left with a 2-0 win, thanks to two breakaway goals by Kenny Cameron.

Celtic refused to panic. Dundee United were crushed 4-0 at Tannadice in the opening league game of the season on Wednesday, 25th August, Joe McBride opening his account, then United were beaten 3-0 at Parkhead in the return League Cup game. Two potentially difficult away hurdles were successfully negotiated in the remaining League Cup sectional games: Motherwell were beaten 3-2 at Fir Park, more comfortably than the scoreline suggests and Dundee went down 3-1 at Dens, this time with less in hand.

The first acid test of Celtic's progress under Stein came at Ibrox on September 18th but Jim Forrest, so often the scourge of Celtic defences, gave Rangers a 1-0 lead in the 7th minute. Celtic levelled through a Hughes penalty eleven minutes later but George McLean scored Rangers' second and winning goal only two minutes later, also from the spot. Rangers managed to contain Celtic's increasingly frantic attacks and held out to win 2-1. Thereafter, the teams ran neck and neck in the League Championship race and both continued their inexorable progress towards a meeting in the League Cup Final. Celtic, having disposed of Raith Rovers 12-1 on aggregate in the two-leg quarter-final, survived a scare in the semi-final against Hibs at Ibrox on October 4th, Lennox scoring a last-gasp equaliser after Neil Martin's two goals had overhauled Joe McBride's 8th minute opener for Celtic. Extra time proved goalless and the replay was set for October 18th at Ibrox, to the furious indignation of both clubs, who justifiably claimed that the winners of the other semi, Rangers or Kilmarnock, would have the advantage of a recent game at Hampden before the final. When the dust had settled, Hibs were swept aside 4-0, Celtic's goals in a thrilling display coming from McBride, Hughes, Lennox and Murdoch.

So it was that on Saturday, October 23rd, at Hampden, the following teams lined up for the final:—

Celtic: Simpson; Young & Gemmell; Murdoch, McNeill & Clark; Johnstone & Gallagher; McBride; Lennox and Hughes.

Rangers: Ritchie; Johansen & Provan; Wood, McKinnon & Greig; Henderson & Willoughby; Forrest; Wilson and Johnston.

The referee, as at the Scottish Cup Final, was Mr Hugh Phillips of Wishaw and even the crowd was the same — 108,000.

This was the game that would **really** show how far Celtic had come. They set out in determined fashion, tackling like tigers for every ball. Rangers, however, settled quicker and Forrest was thwarted by Simpson when the opening goal seemed certain. Rangers' international centre-half, Ron McKinnon, gifted Celtic a penalty kick by reaching up and clutching the ball as it passed over his head for what would have been a harmless goal-kick. Hughes converted the award, sending Ritchie the wrong way.

Ten minutes later, Celtic went 2-0 ahead courtesy of another penalty, awarded when Provan hauled Johnstone down on the bye-line. This time Ritchie could only get a hand to Hughes's drive as it sped past him into the net. The autumn sun was shining for Celtic, who held out in the face of furious Rangers pressure in the second half, with a composure that the pre-Stein teams seldom managed and when Ian Young diverted a Greig header past Simpson six minutes from the end, it was, for Rangers, too little too late.

Unfortunately, Celtic's victory celebrations were marred by a mindless pitch invasion which disrupted their lap of honour. This incident led to a ban on laps of honour which remained in force throughout Jock Stein's time as Celtic manager.

In the meantime, Mr Stein's term as Scotland caretaker manager came to an end in Naples on 7th December. Scotland, having lost two goals in the last seven minutes to go down 2-1 at home to Poland on 13th October and subsequently beaten Italy 1-0 with a last-minute goal from John Greig at Hampden on 9th November, required a draw with Italy to secure a play-off with the 'Azzurri' for a place in the World Cup Finals in England the following summer. Deprived of such stars as Law, Crerand, Baxter, Mackay, Johnstone and Henderson through non-availability and injury, the Scots had virtually no chance of gaining the point they needed and eventually lost 3-0.

Celtic sustained their league challenge and a Happy Christmas was ensured when Morton were crushed 8-1 at Celtic Park, while Dunfermline beat Rangers 3-2 at Ibrox. Early in the New Year, Rangers were trounced 5-1 on an icy Celtic Park, with Hughes running riot, Chalmers scoring a second-half hat-trick and Murdoch and Gallagher rounding off the scoring to eclipse Davy Wilson's second-minute goal for Rangers.

So ended 1965, the year the modern era began for Celtic. Although the Scottish Cup was lost to Rangers by 1-0 in a replayed final and the team lost to Liverpool 2-1 on aggregate in the European Cup Winners' Cup semi-final in controversial circumstances (a good-looking goal by Lennox, which would have put Celtic into the final on the *away goals* rule, was disallowed for offside in the last minute), the season finished with a golden afterglow. The Championship was won, clinched 1-0 at Fir Park after a telegram had been received at Parkhead from Rangers Chairman John Wilson, graciously conceding defeat with the words . . . "The chase is over."

The rest, as they say, is history . . .

After the 1965 Scottish Cup Win

PATSY GALLACHER

THE NAME PATSY GALLACHER is familiar to Celtic supporters of all ages even though his career ended some 60 years ago. Those who watched football before the First World War and throughout the 1920's rated him the greatest player there had ever been or was ever likely to be.

With hindsight this may seem something of an exaggeration but certainly he was the most complete footballer of his era, which is the best to which any player can aspire. His legendary dribbling, passing, tackling and shooting abilities, allied to uncanny ball control and reading of a game made him a man ahead of his time.

At only 5'6" tall and a slender seven stone, it is hardly surprising that manager Willie Maley wondered if the youngster from Donegal had the physical make-up for the hurly-burly of professional football. Nevertheless, having caught the eye of Celtic scouts while playing for Clydebank Juniors, Patsy scored twice in a trial match at Dumfries in 1911. A second trial produced a hat-trick, which clinched his signing.

Though almost pitifully frail, the young Gallacher quickly endeared himself to the fans with his natural ability and class. That first season he secured the first of four Scottish Cup medals, scoring in the final against Clyde.

By the start of World War I, Gallacher was a household name, having been a key figure in the 1914 Double-winning team. While working in the shipyards, he warmed the hearts of the Celtic support throughout the haphazard wartime Scottish League Championships.

Some of Patsy's most celebrated feats were reserved for the 1925 Scottish Cup campaign. Having orchestrated a spectacular 5-0 demolition of Rangers in the semi-final, he conjured up one of Scottish football's all-time-great goals in the final against Dundee. The Taysiders scored in the first-half and clung onto their advantage for much of the second period despite frenzied Celtic pressure. Then Gallacher gained possession and made for the byeline, dodging defender after defender. Evading a final despairing lunge, he cut in towards goal. After being momentarily dispossessed, he recovered the ball, gripped it firmly between his feet and somersaulted over the goal-line — Hampden erupted at this piece of pure wizardry and it seemed almost incidental when Jimmy McGrory headed a routine winner.

That memorable incident proved to be Patsy's Celtic swansong as he became a marked man and increasingly prone to injury. Transferred to Falkirk in 1926, he masterminded The Bairns' quarter-final defeat of Rangers the following year before facing Celtic in the semi, a match marked by the poignant singing of the Parkhead fans: *Will ye no' come back again?*

Patsy Gallacher died in 1953 but the family football tradition was maintained by his sons, who played for Dundee and more recently his grandson, Kevin, of Dundee United, Coventry City and Scotland fame. Amidst speculation that Kevin might one day follow his grandfather to Celtic Park it should be remembered that he would always face unfair comparison with the legend that was Patsy.

Celtic v Hibernian ▼   ▲ *Joe Miller scores against Rangers to win the 1989 Scottish Cup*

CELTIC v Aberdeen
1990 CUP FINAL

AN OPPORTUNITY to finish the season on a real high note. That is what the Tennent's Scottish Cup Final of 1990 was to Celtic, undisputed kings of the country's premier knockout competition in the 102 years since the club was founded.

The task was a formidable one. Lining up against Celtic at Hampden Park on Saturday 12th May were Aberdeen, winners of the Skol Cup and runners-up to Rangers in the Scottish League's Premier Division.

Indeed, many felt that the *Dons* were the best side in the country, key players having recovered from the spate of injuries which had hit the club while in the driving seat in the league in December.

Certainly, their player pool was formidable. Just nine days before the final, Aberdeen had travelled south to Glasgow for their final league game of the season, at Celtic Park. The value of that encounter as a dress rehearsal for the cup showdown was diminished because the *Dons*

fielded a side minus no fewer than seven players virtually certain to feature in the starting eleven for the cup final.

Consternation on the part of Celtic supporters grew dramatically, though, when they saw their side beaten by a comprehensive 3-1 margin by the youthful Aberdeen outfit. What chance had their team against the full strength side, including internationalists Alex McLeish, Jim Bett, Bobby Connor, Charlie Nicholas and deadly Dutchman Hans Gillhaus?

To make matters worse, there were doubts over the fitness of Celtic defenders Paul Elliott and Chris Morris. Elliott had established himself firmly in the affections of the fans with his courageous and totally-committed performances at centre-half and the prospect of trying to contain such as Nicholas and Gillhaus without him was a daunting one.

Similarly, the absence of Morris in earlier games in the season had coincided with two of Celtic's worst defensive displays. He had missed the 5-4

win over Partizan Belgrade through injury and the 3-0 defeat by Rangers because of suspension. So Celtic's bid to win the cup, and secure a place in European competition the following season, was to be made against all odds.

With typical, almost illogical, confidence, most Celtic supporters approached the big day in the belief that their much-maligned side could rise to the occasion once more. A place in the record books, as the first Celtic team to win the competition for a third successive year, beckoned . . . but much more important was to make sure of that Cup Winners' Cup spot.

The pre-match warm-up revealed that Morris had not made it but Elliott was fit. Classy Polish defender Dariusz Wdowczyk was wearing the No. 2 shorts, with Anton Rogan restored at No. 3; but the numbers could not indicate the defensive formation thought up by the Celtic management team. Paul Elliott was the man designated to pick up livewire Gillhaus, while Derek Whyte looked after ex-Celt Nicholas and Rogan kept tabs on the under-rated Paul Mason. That left Wdowczyk, who had played at left-back in his previous 28 appearances in the green-and-white hoops, in a sweeper role behind the three markers.

The early signs were good. The new-look Parkhead defence was in control and Celtic had the lion's share of possession. But over-eagerness almost proved fatal in only the sixth minute. Paul McStay and Billy Stark collided in midfield and Aberdeen snapped up possession. Bett played in a testing cross from the right and this time Elliott and Pat Bonner distracted one another in going for the ball. It broke to Nicholas, playing his final game for Aberdeen and seeking his first winner's medal in national cup competition. The ex-Celt made an opening where most would have failed. He turned and took the ball wide of a defender before firing a low shot past the stranded Bonner.

It looked a certain goal, exactly the sort of early blow which may well have proved fatal to Celtic, so low was their confidence. But Elliott was on the goal-line and stretched out an apparently telescopic right leg to deflect the ball wide for a corner.

The fans breathed a huge, collective sigh of relief and the team settled well. A tight rein was kept on the dangerous Aberdeen front men and some neat football was played further forward. However, the problem which had plagued the side increasingly as the season advanced — an inability to make chances with the invention and regularity associated with Celtic — remained.

Veteran midfielder Billy Stark, surprisingly restored to first-team action at the end of a season which the player had virtually written off through injury, went close with a couple of headers either side of the half-time interval but there were few other signs of a threat to Theo Snelders' goal.

Midway through the second half, the huge army of Celtic supporters produced an incredible wall of sound, reminiscent of the great encouragement which sparked a remarkable fight-back in the 1985 cup final. The players responded and Aberdeen were starved of possession for a spell but still the Celts could not find the spark of inspiration required to break the deadlock.

Extra time seemed inevitable long before the 90 minutes were up, with the spectre of a penalty shoot-out unless one side or the other could produce a deciding goal, either from a flash of inspiration or a fatal error. International priority in World Cup Finals year had played a part in the decision to implement a penalty decider, in the event of the sides being level after 120 minutes, for the first time in the history of the competition.

So it was to be and while it guaranteed a dramatic conclusion to an exciting though rather lack-lustre match, it meant that one side would leave the field devastated . . . and one luckless player in particular.

Celtic were immediately up against it when Wdowczyk sent the first kick wide. Successful kicks by Bett, Connor and Gillhaus kept up the pressure but the full-back's miss was wiped out when Brian Grant fired Aberdeen's fourth over the crossbar. Peter Grant, McStay, and subs Tommy Coyne and Mike Galloway were on target with the remainder of Celtic's opening five kicks.

That left the pressure firmly on Charlie Nicholas. Should he miss the *Dons'* final spot-kick, the cup would go to Celtic and he would be branded forever as the man who missed intentionally to favour his first football love. Instead, he swept his kick into Bonner's postage stamp corner with total conviction.

Joe Miller, Whyte, Elliott and an apparently reluctant Jacki Dziekanowski slotted away the next four Celtic kicks convincingly to keep intense pressure on their Aberdeen counterparts. Alex McLeish, Stewart McKimmie, David Robertson and teenager Graham Watson all converted their penalties impressively, despite the mounting tension.

Amazingly, neither Bonner nor Snelders, arguably the two best 'keepers in the country, had managed to lay a finger on any of the 18 spot-kicks so far, only two of which had been off-target.

Next on the spot for Celtic was defender Anton

Team talk before extra time

Rogan, who had performed splendidly throughout the 120 minutes but whose career has more than once seemed jinxed. The Northern Irish internationalist hit his penalty firmly and true to Snelders' bottom left-hand corner . . . but, for almost the first time, the 'keeper guessed right and got down to make a splendid save.

So Aberdeen's Brian Irvine, the only outfield player still to take a kick, had the chance to clinch a second cup success of the season for his side. He took it, Bonner diving to his right while the ball went slightly to his left.

It was a cruel way to lose a cup, but lose Celtic did. The luckless Rogan was inconsolable but there was dignity in the way the players of each side reacted. Aberdeen captain McLeish offered words of sympathy to several Celts before joining his celebrating team-mates, while Irvine's salute to the Celtic supporters expressed sympathy and admiration for the way the fans remained to hail their beaten heroes.

It was perhaps unfortunate that Aberdeen were limited to a "lap of honour" which only took in the track in front of their own fans, because they would almost certainly have been applauded sportingly by the Celtic supporters who recognised their contribution to the game and to the season as a whole.

As it was, those Celtic fans to their eternal credit, did much to lift their own favourites with a rousing reception when they returned to the pitch after collecting their runners-up medals. One player lingered longer than the others and left bedecked in Celtic scarves. It was none other than Paul Elliott, who had produced yet another magnificent display.

He was not alone. Rogan and Miller were others whose courageous performances delighted the fans, while Wdowczyk's impeccable showing in an unaccustomed position was another major plus.

Still, the numbing reality was that the cup had been lost and a European spot would now depend upon the outcome of the UEFA Cup final and the behaviour of English supporters at the World Cup Finals.

No fewer than eight Celtic players had yet to taste defeat in a Scottish Cup-tie for the club . . . but the silverware was in the hands of Aberdeen.

Not a single goal had been lost in the final six matches played in the competition . . . but another hat-trick bid had ended in cruel failure.

Such were the final bitter-sweet statistics in a campaign of *ifs, buts* and *maybes*.

Great Games

CELTIC v Partizan Belgrade

European Cup-Winners Cup 1st Round

SPECTACULAR MATCHES in European competition have been a feature of the history of Celtic Football Club for almost 30 years but few have been quite as dramatic, if desperately disappointing at the finish, as last season's European Cup-Winners' Cup first round second leg clash with Partizan Belgrade of Yugoslavia.

Played on September 27th 1989, it was the match which saw close season signing Dariusz Dziekanowski elevated to near folk-hero status with a brilliant individual performance in which he scored four goals. Astonishingly, this achievement was not enough to see Celtic into the second round. They won 5-4 on the night but were eliminated on the *away goals* rule, having lost the first leg in Mostar 2-1.

That first leg result had given cause for optimism, in the belief that the vital away goal scored by midfielder Mike Galloway could prove invaluable. It was not to be, as the Celtic defence crumbled alarmingly time and again in the return match at Celtic Park and Dziekanowski's goal-scoring heroics were frustrated.

In hindsight, it could be said that the absence of right-back Chris Morris, through injury, was a vital factor in the defensive uncertainty which plagued the side that night. Manager Billy McNeill fielded captain Roy Aitken in an unfamiliar role as direct replacement for Morris, while Paul Elliott, who had just one first team game in Celtic colours behind him after a beginning to the season ravaged by illness and injury, joined Derek Whyte in the middle of the back four.

The Elliott/Whyte partnership was eventually to emerge as one of the few bright features of a miserable season for the club but it would be fair to say that it had some way to go on the evidence of that night.

Celtic made the worst possible start and lost the advantage of the goal scored in Mostar by conceding one within eight minutes of the start.

Pat Bonner had to look lively to scramble away a shot from Scepovic but the resultant corner was headed powerfully past the keeper by the unmarked Vijacic from just eight yards out. The corner had been taken by midfielder Durovski, who wore black tights under his shorts and was to play an eye-catching role as the night wore on . . . and not just because of his attire.

Andy Walker, who returned to the starting line-up in place of Tommy Coyne, almost levelled matters five minutes later but sent a powerful header skimming inches over the bar from a cross by Joe Miller, another whose place in the starting line-up had been doubtful following a disagreement with the manager over his substitution in the Skol Cup semi-final against Aberdeen a week earlier.

The rough tactics of the visiting side caused anger on the terracings but the Yugoslavs paid for them when Dziekanowski set the crowd alight with a 25th minute equaliser. Paul McStay's free-kick was headed goalwards by Elliott and the Pole raced in to send a header flashing past keeper Pandurovic.

Petric and Spasic were booked for fouls on Mike Galloway as Partizan struggled to contain a Celtic barrage but an Aitken header, just off-target, was the closest they came to taking an interval lead.

Just 80 seconds after the re-start, though, Celtic moved ahead in the match and level on aggregate. Pandurovic fumbled a Peter Grant shot from the edge of the area and Dziekanowski took advantage to blast home the loose ball.

Partizan struck back only four minutes later when Durovski robbed Whyte and set up Dordevic for a simple goal to put them back in the driving seat.

Dziekanowski completed his hat-trick with a right-foot volley which he rifled low past the keeper after Aitken had collected a reverse pass

from Galloway and pulled the ball back from the byeline.

Again the Yugoslavs levelled the match within five minutes when Durovski raced clear to score, East German referee Klaus Peschel ignoring Celtic's appeals for offside.

Celtic clawed themselves in front once more in an incredible second half, with Dziekanowski settling for the role of goal-maker. He mesmerised three defenders wide on the right before sweeping in a superb low cross for Walker to turn the ball past the keeper from point-blank range.

Celtic, though now ahead 4-3 on the night, were only level on goal difference and facing elimination on the *away goals* rule unless they could score again; but 25 minutes remained and their flambuoyant attacking play seemed sure to bring more goals. However, there remained the danger of the loss of further goals as Partizan could hit with deadly effect on the break.

The 49,500 fans threatened to lift the roof off all sections of the ground when Dziekanowski scored his fourth and opened up the necessary two-goal lead just nine minutes from time. He met a left-wing cross from Miller to glance a shot beyond Pandurovic with the outside of his right foot.

Miller then had the chance to kill off the tie a few minutes later but could not make his shooting chance count when Dziekanowski was well placed to score if his fellow-striker had found him with a pass.

Celtic seemed to have done enough but they were dealt a hammer blow when the Yugoslavs notched the vital goal just a minute from the end. The home defence might have cleared at three different stages in the build up, but failed each time. A cross from the Yugoslav left was turned back across goal from beyond the back post and headed past Bonner by Scepovic from six yards out. The keeper's valiant effort to stop the header — he got his fingertips to the ball — did just enough to deflect it beyond the head of Elliott, stationed on the goal-line.

There was no way back for Celtic and fantastic though the entertainment had been, many of the players pinpointed the match as a turning point. It meant elimination from Europe at an early stage yet again and almost certainly had a lasting negative effect on the season . . . but no-one who was at Celtic Park that night, nor the many who watched extended highlights on television, will easily forget the spectacular events of a truly great game.

Jacki Dziekanowski's fourth goal

FUN QUIZZES

1 · General

1. At which ground did Celtic win the League Title in 1972?

2. When Celtic won the double in 1953-'54 who was their captain?

3. What is the worst position that Celtic have finished in the League and in which season?

4. In September 1965, which Irish goalkeeper made his only appearance for Celtic?

5. For which England Internationalist did Celtic play a testimonial in 1970?

6. At which ground did Celtic win the League Title in 1971 and in what circumstances?

7. Who scored Celtic's 7,000th league goal and in which season?

8. Who was the top league scorer for Celtic in 1976-'77 and what was his total?

9. From which club did Celtic sign Bobby Collins in 1948?

10. Who are the last three Celtic players to be named "Scottish Football Writers' Player of the Year"?

2 · Scottish Cup

1. How many times have Celtic won the Scottish Cup?

2. In which year did Celtic first win the Scottish Cup?

3. At which ground was that first cup success achieved?

4. How many of the first 20 Scottish Cup Finals did Celtic win?

5. Apart from war years, what is the longest Celtic have gone without winning the Scottish Cup?

6. How many times have Celtic retained the Scottish Cup?

7. How many Scottish Cup Winner's medals did Billy McNeill achieve as a player?

8. Who was the Celtic goalkeeper in the 1977 Scottish Cup Final victory?

9. Which player played against Celtic in the 1967 final and joined them a decade later?

10. The only two 'hat-tricks' scored in Scottish Cup Finals have been by Celtic players. Name the players and the years.

ANSWERS ON PAGE 64

CHRIS MORRIS

REPUBLIC of Ireland international defender Chris Morris is a player who knows more than most about the uncertainties of football.

January 1st 1986 saw him as a struggling 23-year-old with Sheffield Wednesday and so un-rated by the club's supporters that he was jeered on his appearance as substitute against Norwich City.

Just two years later, the scenario could not have been more contrasting. The intervening 24 months had produced a complete transformation in a career which started with English schoolboy honours for the talented youngster from Newquay, Cornwall.

He was an integral part of a Celtic side which demolished great rivals Rangers in the traditional Ne'erday fixture, setting up both goals in the 2-0 win which pointed the club towards an emphatic league championship triumph in its Centenary Year.

He had also attracted the attention of Republic of Ireland boss Jack Charlton with his consistent and inventive performances in the right-back role.

His versatility was probably the main reason for his failure to make a real breakthrough at Sheffield Wednesday, as he was switched around in a number of positions after making his first team debut in late 1983. As a result, he was never able to hold down a regular position in the side, least of all in the right-back slot held down by local hero Mel Sterland. Most of his 30 league appearances in season 1985/86 came in midfield positions or on the right wing.

He was still a virtual unknown when Celtic manager Billy McNeill signed him for £125,000 in July 1987, in the wake of the departures of four big-name first team stars. More significantly, the legendary Danny McGrain had also left Celtic Park on a free transfer and it was his right-back berth which the boss had earmarked for Morris.

The prospect of taking over from arguably the best full-back in Scottish footballing history was a daunting one but Morris took to it like a duck to water and was undoubtedly one of the major success stories of the fabulous Centenary Season. The popular Cornishman had the distinction of playing in every competitive game — 51 in total — and his reliability and consistency helped to give the side a defensive stability rarely seen in the previous 20 years.

His impressive form also led to an international call-up by the Republic of Ireland towards the end of the season, his Irish mother providing the qualification for a country which was not that of his birth.

Since his debut appearance, his international career has blossomed in tandem with the fortunes of the Republic of Ireland on a world scale. So much so that the player has appeared on the biggest stages available to a European player: the European Nations' Championship Finals in West Germany in 1988 and the 1990 World Cup Finals in Italy.

On both occasions, he performed with the composure and consistency which Celtic supporters have come to expect and the indications are that he will add many more caps to the present tally of over 20.

Further success on the domestic front can also be anticipated. To the league championship and Scottish Cup winner's medals earned in the 1987-88 season, he added a second Scottish Cup success the following season after making a remarkably swift recovery from appendicitis to take his place in the final.

That brief illness had finally broken his remarkable record of neary 100 consecutive appearances since signing for Celtic but the disappointment of missing out on a century was erased by the Hampden defeat of a Rangers side chasing a domestic treble.

Chris looks likely to remain an integral part of both the Celtic and Republic of Ireland sides for some years to come.

Career Statistics

Season	League		League Cup		Scottish Cup		Europe		Total	
	Apps	Goals	Apps	Goals	Apps	Goals	Apps	Goals	Apps	Goals
87-88	44	3	3		6		2		55	3
88-89	33	3	3		4		4		44	3
89-90	32	1	4		5	1	1		42	2
Total	109	7	10		15	1	7		141	8

Numbers in brackets indicate additional appearances as substitute.

Jacki Dziekanowski scores against Rangers August 1989

JOHN THOMSON

CELTIC have produced many legends on the playing field but none generates more emotion than John Thomson. For Thomson is revered by many in much the same way as those who lost their lives in battle because he died while playing for the club.

John Thomson was born in Kirkcaldy in 1909, but moved to Cardenden with his family shortly after World War I. It was there that he began his football career in earnest, joining the famous Wellesley Juniors. He was spotted by Celtic Scout Steve Callaghan who was so impressed that he signed him on the strength of one performance.

The chance to demonstrate his prowess in goal first came on February 12th 1927 in a league match against Dundee. The 17-year-old was called up to the senior side from the reserves when regular goalkeeper Shevlin's loss of three goals the week before led manager Willie Maley to favour the introduction of youth.

Thomson, as is so often the case with a youngster making his debut, started edgily but rallied to produce a tremendous second-half display. He retained his place the following week and for the remainder of the season, producing several scintillating displays which built him a tremendous reputation and won him a Scottish Cup medal at the end of that campaign.

Such was the regard in which he was held that he became known as the '*Prince of Goalkeepers*' and international recognition came his way in 1930 against France, Scotland winning 2-0. His international career blossomed and he played against all the home countries the following season, performing with great distinction and losing only one goal in three matches.

Further success came his way on the domestic front when Celtic again won the Scottish Cup at the climax of the 1930-31 season and Thomson looked set to go on to even greater things when a 1931-32 pre-season USA tour saw him in sparkling form.

Fate was then to intervene. On September 5 1931 against Rangers at Ibrox, the 22-year-old keeper courageously dived at the feet of Rangers striker Sam English and suffered such a serious head injury that he died the same evening in the city's Victoria Infirmary.

The scenes at his funeral have become almost as legendary as the man himself. An estimated 30,000 people lined the mile-long funeral route in Cardenden while some 20,000 more gathered in Queen Street station to watch the mourners leave. Special trains, buses and cars ferried the thousands to Fife with some even making the journey on foot.

It is impossible to say what John Thomson may have achieved or what heights his career may have reached but newspaper and eye-witness accounts support the widely-held view that his was a truly remarkable talent.

Career Statistics

Season	League		League Cup		Scottish Cup		Europe		Total	
	Apps	Goals	Apps	Goals	Apps	Goals	Apps	Goals	Apps	Goals
85-86	11								11	
86-87	42		5		4		3		54	
87-88	41	3	2		5		2	1	50	4
88-89	20(2)		1(1)		2		3		26(3)	
89-90	35	1	3		6		2		46	1
Total	149(2)	4	11(1)		17		10	1	187(3)	5

Numbers in brackets indicate additional appearances as substitute.

DEREK WHYTE

HAVING been part of the first team set-up for almost five years it is hard to believe that Derek Whyte is still what might be termed a young player. For his senior side experience and mature play on the park bear all the hallmarks of, if not quite a veteran, then certainly an experienced performer.

This is less surprising on closer examination of his Celtic career. For, since making his debut as a 17-year-old on February 22nd 1986 in a 1-1 draw with Hearts at Celtic Park, Derek has been an automatic choice for the first team. Only injury or, on very rare occasions suspension, has prevented him from taking his place in the starting line-up.

It has been a remarkable record for a young man whose Celtic career can be traced back to his time with Celtic Boys' Club at under-16 level. He quickly progressed to the point where he signed for the senior club in 1985.

Less than a year later he was performing in the top team and he played the final 11 league games of the remarkable 1985-86 season when Celtic won their 34th league title in the most dramatic of circumstances, pipping Hearts on goal difference in the final league game, which saw them demolishing St Mirren 5-0, while Hearts contributed to their own demise by losing 2-0 at Dundee.

Derek made further progress the following season, playing 54 times in a year of near misses and ultimate disappointments as Celtic finished runners-up in both the league and League Cup to Rangers. Whyte's continued development was one of the few bright spots of the time as, even at such an early stage in his career, he was proving himself a skilful and composed defender. Always more likely to play the ball out of defence than simply boot it to safety, his play is also devoid of the cynicism and aggression associated with many defenders.

He received a Scotland call-up during the 1986-87 season, making his debut for Scotland's under-21s against the Republic of Ireland and retaining his position for the season's remaining four internationals at the age group.

Personal milestones, as well as the obvious successes for the club in its Centenary Year, abounded in the 1987-88 campaign. He clocked up his 100th first team appearance for the club and was one of the lynchpins of a superb defence which lost only 23 goals in 44 games on the way to the championship. He also collected his first Scottish Cup winner's medal and made his full international debut against Belgium — all this while still only 19 years old.

Derek's ever-increasing worth to the Celtic side was shown the following season when he missed almost two months of the programme and Celtic's challenge for the title crumbled amidst defensive frailties. He returned to collect his second Scottish Cup winner's medal on a glorious day in May, producing an outstanding display at the heart of the Celtic defence alongside Mick McCarthy in the 1-0 victory over treble-chasing *Old Firm* rivals Rangers.

During a year of almost unrelenting gloom on the pitch, the performances of Derek Whyte last season were among the crumbs of comfort for the fans. The Cumbernauld-born defender continued to mature into undoubtedly one of the country's top players.

Just 22 in August, Whyte has time to realise the enormous potential which took him so close to representing Scotland in the World Cup in Italy and seems sure to make him one of Scotland's stalwarts come the 1994 tournament in America.

Celebr

ations

ITALIA 90

The Celtic Connection

THE INVOLVEMENT of Celtic Football Club in the 1990 World Cup Finals ended with the Republic of Ireland's 1-0 quarter-final defeat by host nation, Italy, in Rome. But it was with pride triumphant over disappointment that the great Italian adventure closed for the Republic and its vast army of immaculately-behaved fans.

Celtic stars Pat Bonner and Chris Morris certainly emerged with their reputations significantly enhanced.

Goalkeeper Bonner was possibly the side's most-talked-about performer, especially after the *penalty shoot-out* save which secured victory over Romania in the last 16. The consistency of his displays over the Republic's five matches was simply confirmation of the fact that he undoubtedly now ranks among the best half-dozen 'keepers in the world.

Ireland had played less than 10 minutes of World Cup Finals football when England's Gary

Lineker opened his country's account with a strike which owed a great deal to good fortune. Doubters believed the 'underdogs' would fold if they fell behind early on to quality opposition — but nothing could have been further from the truth. The Irish continued to play with conviction and their late equaliser from Kevin Sheedy was long overdue and scant reward for a match they dominated.

Indeed, such was their dominance in the match that Bonner was not seriously tested and Morris was seen more in the attacking role so familiar to Celtic supporters than in the defensive berth of a right-back. Chris's constant availability wide in attack is a key feature of the Republic's game plan and his tidy use of the ball and accuracy in crossing were much in evidence throughout the campaign.

Bonner conceded a second goal in the group matches when Holland and Ruud Gullit in particular at last found some of the form which had made them European Champions two years earlier; but again the Irish fought back from the loss of an early goal and some dubious decisions against them to fully merit the 1-1 draw which earned a place in the knockout stages.

So sound was the defensive barrier erected by the Irish and marshalled by ex-Celt Mick McCarthy in quite magnificent fashion, that Bonner had relatively few opportunities to demonstrate his ability in the group games — but it was a different story once the sudden-death matches got underway.

The Republic of Ireland lined up against a Romanian side which had proved itself to be one of the most talented in the competition. In midfielder Gheorge Hagi, they had possibly the most gifted individual on display.

The Irish were more seriously tested in this match than by any of their previous opponents and Bonner was called upon to make two top-class saves in the second half. The second, from Hagi, almost defied belief. They had their chances, too, but a *penalty shoot-out* seemed on the cards throughout extra time following the goalless 90 minutes.

Celtic fans were fairly confident of the outcome. Bonner had been unable to lay a hand on any of Aberdeen's 10 spot-kicks in the Scottish Cup Final and could surely not suffer such bad luck again.

So it proved, as he made a magnificent diving save to prevent substitute Timofte from converting the Romanians' fifth kick and give David O'Leary the chance to slot away the vital penalty, which he duly did quite convincingly.

Success ensured a quarter-final spot for the Republic and though hosts Italy represented the most formidable opposition imaginable, no-one was to be disappointed.

Apart from the match itself, a highlight of the Irish stay in Rome came when some of the squad met Polish ex-goalkeeper, Karol Wojtyla — better known as *Pope John Paul II!*

Not that the Papal Audience distracted them from the task in hand. The Republic went on to give Italy a rougher ride than any of the hosts' earlier opponents, despite losing out to a single goal scored late in the first half after Bonner had blocked a ferocious shot from Donadoni. The big 'keeper was unlucky to stumble as he made the save and Italian scoring sensation Schillaci had the opening and the composure to steer the rebound into the unprotected net.

The Italians were forced back for long periods of the second half and did not enjoy the experience; but the Portuguese referee denied the Irish a chance to exert greater pressure by penalising them for the slightest physical contact.

However, in the end, the Italians were worthy winners — only a fantastic late save by 'Packy' prevented Serena from making it 2-0 — and the Irish contingent set off for home with heads held high.

SADLY, the Scotland squad could not match the Republic's heroics, though they were not disgraced and once more came agonisingly close to advancing to the second phase for the first time in the country's history.

The opening 1-0 defeat by Costa Rica was certainly the fatal blow and a cruel one at that. For the Scots dominated and had half-a-dozen clear scoring chances but just could not beat an inspired 'keeper.

The wonderful Scottish fans got something to cheer about with a courageous, nail-biting 2-1 victory over Sweden. But the challenge of taking a point from mighty Brazil to qualify was just too much and other group results denied Scotland even a *best-third-place* spot in the last 16.

Paul McStay was the only current Celtic player in the squad, though he was joined by several ex-Celts on the playing side as well as various club officials and backroom staff in the S.F.A. party.

Chairman Jack McGinn was present as Treasurer of the Association. Vice-chairman Kevin Kelly was also there as a member of the management committee of the Scottish Football League.

First-team coach Tommy Craig was one of Andy Roxburgh's key assistants and masseur Jimmy Steel occupied the same role with Scotland as he does at Celtic Park.

Last but not least, teenage Celtic starlet, Brian O'Neil, was one of the Scotland under-16 squad rewarded for their contribution to the nation's magnificent run in the World Youth Cup last year with a place in the travelling party for Italy.

Roll on U.S.A. 1994!

Triumphant Lisbon Lions

CLUB HONOURS

EUROPEAN CUP: 1967.

LEAGUE CHAMPIONS (35 times)
1893, 1894, 1896, 1898, 1905, 1906, 1907, 1908,
1909, 1910, 1914, 1915, 1916, 1917, 1919, 1922,
1926, 1936, 1938, 1954, 1966, 1967, 1968, 1969,
1970, 1971, 1972, 1973, 1974, 1977, 1979, 1981,
1982, 1986, 1988.

SCOTTISH CUP WINNERS (29 times)
1892, 1899, 1900, 1904, 1907, 1908, 1911, 1912,
1914, 1923, 1925, 1927, 1931, 1933, 1937, 1951,
1954, 1965, 1967, 1969, 1971, 1972, 1974, 1975,
1977, 1980, 1985, 1988, 1989.

LEAGUE CUP WINNERS (9 times)
1957, 1958, 1966, 1967, 1968, 1969, 1970, 1975,
1982.

EMPIRE EXHIBITION CUP: 1938.

ST. MUNGO CUP: 1951.

CORONATION CUP: 1953.

RECORD VICTORY: 11-0 v Dundee (Division 1),
October 1895.

**MOST INDIVIDUAL LEAGUE GOALS IN A
SEASON:** 50 James McGrory (1935-36).

HIGHEST AGGREGATE SCORER: James
McGrory 397 (1922-1939).

MOST CAPPED PLAYER: Danny McGrain, 62
times for Scotland.

SEASON'S FACTS & FIGURES

Date	Comp.	Opposition	Score	Crowd	1	2	3	4	5	6
1989										
19 July	F	Rheydter (A)	0-0	n/a	Bonner	Grant	Rogan	McCahill	P. Elliott	Whyte
21 July	F	Kickers Offenbach (A)	0-0	n/a	Bonner	Morris	Rogan	Aitken	McCahill	Whyte
22 July	F	Borussia M'gladbach (A)	1-4	n/a	Andrews	Morris	Rogan	Aitken	P. Elliott	Whyte
24 July	F	Hohenlinberg (A)	4-2	n/a	Andrews	Morris	Rogan	Aitken	P. Elliott	Whyte
30 July	F	Buckie Thistle (A)	3-0	n/a	Bonner	Morris	Rogan	Aitken	Whyte	Grant
1 Aug.	F	Inverness Caledonian (A)	3-0	n/a	Bonner	Morris	Rogan	Aitken	McCahill	Grant
5 Aug.	F	Dynamo Moscow (H)	2-2	35,657	Bonner	Morris	Rogan	Aitken	Whyte	Grant
12 Aug.	PD	Heart of Midlothian (A)	3-1	26,968	Bonner	Morris	Burns	Aitken	Whyte	Grant
15 Aug.	LC	Dumbarton (A)	3-0	9,000	Bonner	Morris	Burns •	Aitken	Whyte	Grant
19 Aug.	PD	Dunfermline Athletic (H)	1-0	34,000	Bonner	Morris	Burns	Aitken	Whyte	Grant
22 Aug.	LC	Queen of the South (H)	2-0	21,062	Bonner	Morris	Rogan	Aitken	Whyte	Grant •
26 Aug.	PD	Rangers (H)	1-1	54,000	Bonner	Morris	Burns	Aitken	Whyte	Grant •
30 Aug.	LC (QF)	Heart of Midlothian (A)	2-2*	26,847	Bonner	Morris	Burns	Aitken	Whyte	Grant
9 Sept.	PD	St Mirren (A)	0-1	19,291	Bonner	Morris	Burns	Aitken	Whyte	Grant
12 Sept.	ECWC	Partizan Belgrade (A)	1-2	15,000	Bonner	Morris	Rogan	Aitken	Whyte	Grant
16 Sept.	PD	Dundee United (A)	2-2	16,454	Bonner	Morris •	Rogan	Aitken	Whyte	McCah
20 Sept.	LC (SF)	Aberdeen (N)	0-1	45,492	Bonner	Morris	Rogan	Aitken	McCahill	Burns
23 Sept.	PD	Motherwell (H)	1-1	29,000	Bonner	Morris	Rogan	Whyte	P. Elliott	Grant
27 Sept.	ECWC	Partizan Belgrade (H)	5-4	49,500	Bonner	Grant	Rogan	Aitken	P. Elliott	Whyte
30 Sept.	PD	Aberdeen (A)	1-1	22,500	Bonner	Morris	Rogan	Aitken	P. Elliott	Whyte
4 Oct.	PD	Hibernian (H)	3-1	36,000	Bonner	Morris	Rogan	Aitken	P. Elliott	Whyte
14 Oct.	PD	Dundee (A)	3-1	16,456	Bonner	Morris	Rogan	Aitken •	P. Elliott	Whyte
21 Oct.	PD	Heart of Midlothian (H)	2-1	40,500	Bonner	Morris	Burns	Aitken •	P. Elliott	Whyte
28 Oct.	PD	Dunfermline Athletic (A)	0-2	19,580	Bonner	Morris	Rogan	Aitken	P. Elliott	Whyte
4 Nov.	PD	Rangers (A)	0-1	41,598	Bonner	Morris	Burns	Aitken	P. Elliott	Whyte
14 Nov.	F	Raith Rovers (A)	2-1	n/a	Andrews	Balmer	Rogan	Grant	P. Elliott	McCah
18 Nov.	PD	Dundee United (H)	0-1	32,350	Bonner	Morris	Burns	Rogan	P. Elliott	Fulton
22 Nov.	PD	St Mirren (H)	1-1	23,100	Bonner	Morris	Rogan	Wdowczyk	P. Elliott	Whyte
25 Nov.	PD	Motherwell (A)	0-0	16,069	Bonner	Morris	Rogan	Wdowczyk	P. Elliott	Whyte
2 Dec.	PD	Aberdeen (H)	1-0	38,300	Bonner	Morris	Wdowczyk	Aitken	P. Elliott	Whyte
6 Dec.	F	Ajax Amsterdam (H)	1-0	20,166	Bonner	Grant	Wdowczyk	Aitken •	P. Elliott	Whyte
9 Dec.	PD	Hibernian (A)	3-0	17,500	Bonner	Morris	Wdowczyk •	Aitken	P. Elliott	Whyte
16 Dec.	PD	Dundee (H)	4-1	17,860	Bonner	Morris	Wdowczyk	Aitken	Rogan	Whyte
26 Dec.	PD	Heart of Midlothian (A)	0-0	23,259	Bonner	Morris	Wdowczyk	Aitken	P. Elliott	Whyte
30 Dec.	PD	Dunfermline Athletic (H)	0-2	30,548	Bonner	Morris	Wdowczyk	Aitken	P. Elliott	Whyte
1990										
2 Jan.	PD	Rangers (H)	0-1	54,000	Bonner	Morris	Wdowczyk	Aitken	P. Elliott	Whyte
6 Jan.	PD	St Mirren (A)	2-0	13,813	Bonner	Galloway	Wdowczyk	Aitken	P. Elliott	Whyte
13 Jan.	PD	Dundee United (A)	0-2	16,635	Bonner	Morris	Wdowczyk	Galloway	P. Elliott	Whyte
20 Jan.	SC	Forfar Athletic (A)	2-1	8,388	Bonner	Morris • (P)	Wdowczyk	Galloway	McCahill	Whyte
27 Jan.	PD	Motherwell (H)	0-1	23,000	Bonner	Morris	Wdowczyk	Galloway	Rogan	Whyte
3 Feb.	PD	Dundee (A)	0-0	14,100	Bonner	Morris	Wdowczyk	Galloway	P. Elliott	Whyte
10 Feb.	PD	Hibernian (H)	1-1	25,000	Bonner	Morris	Wdowczyk	Galloway	P. Elliott	Whyte
17 Feb.	PD	Aberdeen (A)	1-1	22,500	Bonner	Morris	Wdowczyk	Galloway	P. Elliott	Whyte
25 Feb.	SC	Rangers (H)	1-0	52,565	Bonner	Morris	Wdowczyk	Galloway	P. Elliott	Whyte
3 March	PD	Dundee United (H)	3-0	23,541	Bonner	Morris	Wdowczyk	Galloway •	P. Elliott	Whyte
10 March	PD	Heart of Midlothian (H)	1-1	34,792	Bonner	Morris	Wdowczyk	Galloway	P. Elliott	Whyte
17 March	SC (QF)	Dunfermline Athletic (A)	0-0	19,568	Bonner	Morris	Wdowczyk	Rogan	P. Elliott	Whyte
21 March	SC (QFR)	Dunfermline Athletic (H)	3-0	40,798	Bonner	Morris	Wdowczyk	Rogan	P. Elliott	Whyte
24 March	PD	Dunfermline Athletic (A)	0-0	14,044	Bonner	Morris	Wdowczyk	Rogan	P. Elliott	Whyte
31 March	PD	Rangers (A)	0-3	41,926	Bonner	Grant	Wdowczyk	Rogan	P. Elliott	Whyte
7 April	PD	St Mirren (H)	0-3	18,481	Bonner	Morris	Wdowczyk	Galloway	McCahill	Whyte
14 April	SC (SF)	Clydebank (N)	2-0	34,768	Bonner	Morris	Wdowczyk	Fulton	Galloway	Whyte
17 April	PD	Hibernian (A)	0-1	12,000	Bonner	Morris	Wdowczyk	Galloway	Rogan	Whyte
21 April	PD	Dundee (H)	1-1	15,115	Bonner	Morris	Wdowczyk	Grant	P. Elliott	Whyte
28 April	PD	Motherwell (A)	1-1	10,322	Bonner	Galloway	Wdowczyk	Grant	Rogan	Whyte
5 May	PD	Aberdeen (H)	1-3	20,154	Bonner	Galloway	Wdowczyk	Grant	Rogan	Whyte
12 May	SC (F)	Aberdeen (N)	0-0**	60,493	Bonner	Wdowczyk	Rogan	Grant	P. Elliott	Whyte

ABBREVIATIONS:

F = Friendly
PD = Premier Division
LC = League Cup
SC = Scottish Cup
ECWC = European Cup Winners' Cup
QF = Quarter Final
QFR = QF Replay
SF = Semi-final
F = Final

H/A/N = Home/Away/Neutral
* = Penalty Shoot-out, Celtic won 3-1
** = Penalty Shoot-out, Celtic lost 9-8
• = Goal
•(P) = Penalty Goal
(1), (7), (10) etc. = (No.) of player substituted
n/a = not available

Celtic score shown first in Score column.

Peter Grant   Paul Elliott

7	8	9	10	11	12	13	Other substitutes
iot	McStay	Walker	Fulton	Burns	Andrews (1)	Morris (5)	Galloway (11)
way	McStay	Dziekanowski	Walker	Grant	Andrews (1)	Burns (3)	Fulton (7), D. Elliot (10)
way	McStay	Dziekanowski	Coyne	Burns	Fulton (7)	Walker (8) ● (P)	
way ●	McStay	Coyne ●●	Walker	Fulton	Grant (2)	Burns (6)	D. Elliot (8), Dziekanowski (10) ●
e	Fulton	Dziekanowski	Coyne	Burns ●●	Balmer (2)	Walker (9)	
e	McStay	Dziekanowski ●	Walker ●	Burns ●	Balmer (5)	Fulton (8)	Coyne (10)
way	McStay	Dziekanowski ●	Coyne ● (P)	Burns	Mathie (7)	Walker (10)	Fulton (11)
way	McStay	Dziekanowski ●	Coyne ● (P) ●●	Fulton	Rogan	Walker (9)	
way ●	McStay ●	Dziekanowski ●	Coyne	Hewitt	Rogan (8)	Walker (9)	
way	McStay	Dziekanowski	Walker	Hewitt	Fulton	Coyne	
way	McStay	Dziekanowski ●	Coyne	Hewitt	Rogan	Walker	
way	McStay	Dziekanowski	Coyne	Hewitt	Rogan	Walker (11) ●	
way	McStay	Dziekanowski	Coyne	Hewitt	Rogan (3)	Walker	
way ●	McStay	Dziekanowski	Coyne	Burns	Andrews	Walker (9)	Miller, Fulton, McCahill
way	McStay	Dziekanowski	Coyne ●	Fulton	Walker (9)	Miller	
way	McStay	Dziekanowski	Coyne	Fulton	Miller (11)	Walker (12)	
way	McStay ●	Dziekanowski	Coyne	Fulton	Walker (10)	Burns	
way	McStay	Dziekanowski ●●	Walker ●	Miller	Andrews	Burns	Coyne, Fulton, McCahill
way	McStay	Dziekanowski	Walker	Miller ●	Burns	Coyne	
way	McStay	Dziekanowski ●	Walker ●(P)●(P)	Miller	Burns	Coyne	
way	McStay	Dziekanowski ●	Walker	Mathie	Burns (8)	Coyne (10) ●	
way	McStay	Dziekanowski	Walker	Mathie	Coyne (10) ●	Miller (11)	
way	McStay	Dziekanowski	Coyne	Miller	Walker (11)	Grant	
way	McStay	Dziekanowski	Coyne	Miller	Walker (9)	Grant	
way	Fulton ●	Coyne	Walker ● (P)	Hewitt	McLaughlin	Burns	Mathie, McCarrison
way	McStay	Dziekanowski	Walker	Miller	Hewitt (11)	Grant (10)	
	McStay	Dziekanowski	Walker	Miller ●	Hewitt (11)	Galloway (4)	
	McStay	Dziekanowski	Walker	Miller	Hewitt (11)	Galloway (3)	
t	McStay	Dziekanowski	Walker ● (P)	Hewitt	Galloway (10)	Miller	
t	Galloway	Coyne	Walker	Burns	McStay (4)	Rogan (6)	Miller (7), Dziekanowski (10)
t	Galloway	Dziekanowski ●	Walker ●	Hewitt	Fulton	Coyne	Fulton (11)
t	McStay ●	Dziekanowski ●	Walker ●	Hewitt	Galloway (5)	Miller (11) ●	
way	McStay	Dziekanowski ●	Walker	Hewitt	Grant (7)	Coyne (9)	
t	McStay	Dziekanowski	Walker	Hewitt	Coyne (7)	Miller (10)	
	McStay	Coyne	Galloway	Miller	Walker (10)	Dziekanowski (11)	
e	McStay	Dziekanowski ●	Fulton	Miller ●	Walker (7)	Hewitt (9)	
ie	McStay	Dziekanowski ●	Fulton	Miller	Walker (7)	Grant	
ie	McStay	Dziekanowski ●	Fulton	Miller	Walker (7)	Grant	
-	McStay	Dziekanowski	Walker	Fulton	Coyne (10)	D. Elliot (7)	
	McStay	Dziekanowski	Coyne	Rogan	Fulton (7)	Walker (10)	
	McStay	Dziekanowski ●	Coyne	Fulton	Miller (4)	Walker (10)	
	McStay ●	Dziekanowski	Coyne	Fulton	Miller (11)	Walker	
	McStay	Dziekanowski	Coyne ●	Miller	Rogan	Walker (10)	
	McStay	Dziekanowski	Coyne ●	Miller ●	Rogan	Walker	
	McStay	Dziekanowski	Coyne ●	Miller	Rogan	Walker (9)	
	McStay	Dziekanowski	Coyne ●	Miller	Fulton	Walker	
t	McStay ●	Dziekanowski	Coyne ●	Miller ●	Fulton	Walker (11)	
	McStay	Walker	Coyne	Creaney	Mathie (10)	Fulton (4)	
way	McStay	Dziekanowski	Coyne	Miller	Fulton (4)	Walker (9)	
t	McStay	Walker	Coyne	Miller	D. Elliot (11)	Creaney (9)	
t	McStay	Dziekanowski	Walker ●●	Miller	Rogan	Coyne	
	McStay	Creaney	Walker	Fulton	Dziekanowski (7)	Miller (4)	
ie	McStay	Miller	Walker	Fulton	Rogan (11)	Creaney (9) ●	
	McStay	Dziekanowski ●	Walker	Fulton	Miller (9)	Creaney (10)	
	McStay	Dziekanowski	Walker ●	Fulton	Miller (11)	Creaney (7)	
	McStay	Dziekanowski	Walker	Miller	Galloway (7)	Coyne (10)	

riusz Wdowczyk

Jacki Dziekanowski

Paul McStay

FIRST-TEAM STATISTICS '89/90

Player	Premier Division		League Cup		Scottish Cup		Europe		Others		Totals	
	Apps.	Goals	Apps.	Goals	Apps.	Goals	Apps.	Goals	Apps.	Goals	Apps.	Goals
P. Bonner	36	9/37	4	2/3	6	5/1 + 9P	2	-/6	6	5/2	54	21/58
P. McStay	35	3	4	1	6	1	2	—	6 (1)	—	53 (1)	5
D. Whyte	35	1	3	—	6	—	2	—	7	—	53	1
D. Dziekanowski	31 (2)	8	4	3	6	1	2	4	5 (2)	3	48 (4)	19
C. Morris	32	1	4	—	5	1	1	—	6 (1)	—	48 (1)	2
M. Galloway	29 (4)	2	4	—	3 (1)	—	2	1	5 (1)	1	43 (6)	4
P. Grant	24 (2)	—	3	1	5	—	2	—	7 (1)	—	41 (3)	1
P. Elliott	25	—	—	—	4	—	1	—	5	—	35	—
A. Rogan	17 (2)	—	2 (1)	—	3	—	2	—	8	—	32 (3)	—
R. Aitken	18	2	4	—	—	—	2	—	7	1	31	3
T. Coyne	17 (6)	7	3	—	3 (1)	2	1	—	6 (1)	3	30 (8)	12
D. Wdowczyk	23	1	—	—	6	—	—	—	1	—	30	1
A. Walker	19 (13)	6	1 (3)	1	2 (3)	2	1 (1)	1	6 (3)	4	29 (23)	14
J. Miller	16 (8)	5	(1)	—	6	1	1	—	(1)	—	23 (10)	6
S. Fulton	13 (2)	—	1 (1)	—	2	—	—	—	4 (5)	1	20 (8)	1
T. Burns	7 (1)	—	3	1	—	—	1	—	6 (3)	3	17 (4)	4
J. Hewitt	8 (4)	—	3	—	—	—	—	—	2	—	13 (4)	—
A. Mathie	5 (1)	—	—	—	—	—	1	—	2 (2)	—	8 (3)	—
S. McCahill	2	—	1	—	1	—	—	—	4	—	8	—
B. Stark	2	—	—	—	1	—	—	—	1	—	4	—
I. Andrews	—	—	—	—	—	—	—	—	3 (2)	-/7	3 (2)	-/7
G. Creaney	2 (4)	1	—	—	—	—	—	—	—	—	2 (4)	1
D. Elliot	(2)	—	—	—	—	—	—	—	1 (2)	—	1 (4)	—
S. Balmer	—	—	—	—	—	—	—	—	1 (2)	—	1 (2)	—
D. McCarrison	—	—	—	—	—	—	—	—	(1)	—	(1)	—
?. Mclaughlin	—	—	—	—	—	—	—	—	(1)	—	(1)	—

Numbers in brackets indicate additional appearances as substitute. For P. Bonner and I. Andrews, figures in Goals column represent Shut-outs/Goals Conceded (P = Penalties in Cup Final Shoot-out).

FUN QUIZ ANSWERS

CELTIC IN THE SCOTTISH CUP

1. 29 times.
2. 1892.
3. Ibrox.
4. Only 1.
5. 10 Years (1955-1964 inclusive).
6. 6 times.
7. Seven.
8. Peter Latchford.
9. Frank Munro.
10. Jimmy Quinn (1904) and 'Dixie' Deans (1972).

GENERAL QUIZ

1. Bayview, Methil.
2. Jock Stein.
3. 12th (Season 1947/48).
4. John Kennedy.
5. Bobby Moore.
6. Hampden (v. Ayr Utd.) — because of ground reconstruction at Celtic Park.
7. Brian McClair (Season 1985/86).
8. Ronnie Glavin (19 goals).
9. Pollok Juniors.
10. Paul McStay (1987/88); Brian McClair (1986/87); Charlie Nicholas (1982/83).

ACKNOWLEDGEMENTS

Published by Holmes McDougall Limited, Allander House, 137-141 Leith Walk, Edinburgh EH6 8NS, Scotland.

Printed and bound in Scotland.
Design & Artwork by *David C. Wilson*.
Principal Writers: Donald Cowey and Andrew Smith ('The Celtic View').
Photographs supplied by *Celtic Football Club*, *The Glaswegian* and *The Evening Times*.
Edited by John Traynor and Douglas Russell (Holmes McDougall Limited).

Every effort has been made by the publishers to ensure the accuracy of all details and information in this publication.